Portable UNIX™

Douglas W. Topham

John Wiley & Sons

New York • Chichester • Brisbane • Toronto • Singapore

This publication is designed to provide accurate and authoritative information in regard to the subject matter covered. It is sold with the understanding that the publisher is not engaged in rendering legal, accounting, or other professional service. If legal advice or other expert assistance is required, the services of a competent professional person should be sought. FROM A DECLARATION OF PRINCIPLES JOINTLY ADOPTED BY A COMMITTEE OF THE AMERICAN BAR ASSOCIATION AND A COMMITTEE OF PUBLISHERS.

Library of Congress Cataloging-in-Publication Data

Topham, Douglas W., 1942-
     Portable UNIX/Douglas W. Topham.
        p.   cm.
     Includes index.
     ISBN 0-471-57926-2 (alk. paper)
     1. Operating systems (Computers) 2. UNIX (Computer file)
     I. Title.
     QA76.76.O63T666   1992
     005.4'3--dc20   92-24561
                                           CIP

Printed in the United States of America
10 9 8 7 6 5 4 3 2 1

Contents

Contents

Introduction

Portable UNIX is an easy-to-use reference for UNIX commands, options, directories, and files. It provides essential information on the most commonly used commands.

This book is mainly for beginners, although experienced UNIX users can also use it. It assumes that your UNIX software is already installed and that you are reasonably familiar with basic procedures.

Have you forgotten the name of a command? The syntax of its command line? The steps of a procedure to follow? This book gives you step-by-step instructions for using a command without inundating you with unnecessary technical information. Use this book to look up the name of a command, its syntax, or the steps for using it. The book is compact and easy to use. If you need more detailed information, you can refer to the complete UNIX documentation.

Version of UNIX

This book covers UNIX System V, Release 4. This release incorporates the most popular features of UNIX System V, XENIX System V, and Berkeley BSD 4.2. It has been ported to microcomputers, workstations, minicomputers, and mainframes made by IBM, DEC, AT&T, Hewlett-Packard, Sun Microsystems, Apple, and many others. Although there may be some variations from one system to another, most of the information in this book should apply to your system.

Organization of This Book

Portable UNIX is divided into eight chapters and five appendices. The first chapter deals with basic concepts. The next seven cover commands that relate to various types of activities. The appendices provide the names of commonly used directories and files, along with programming information. The chapters on commands are arranged alphabetically by command function.

Chapter 1, "UNIX Concepts," discusses basic procedures, such as entering a command line, redirecting input and output, and using pipes.

Chapter 2, "General-Purpose Utilities," describes utilities that perform elementary functions, such as displaying the date and time, changing to a different directory, terminating a process, or displaying a calendar.

Chapter 3, "File Handling," describes the utilities that you use to work with files, such as those that enable you to display the contents of a file; copy, move, rename, delete, or find a file; check spelling; or display the names of files in a directory.

Chapter 4, "Text- and Number-Processing," shows you how to perform numerical calculations, search for text, search and replace, sort, and reformat.

Chapter 5, "Text Editing and Formatting," covers the programs that you use to create files, enter text, and format it for printing.

Chapter 6, "Printing," discusses the various commands that you use to print a document, display the status of the printer, cancel a printing job, or convert text from one printer type to another.

Chapter 7, "Communications," covers the commands that you use to communicate with other users on your own UNIX system or on another.

Chapter 8, "System Administration," provides those commands that a system administrator uses to take care of the hardware, software, and users on a UNIX system.

Appendix A, "The UNIX Locator," tells you where to find various directories and files.

Appendix B, "The Bourne Shell," describes shell programming with the Bourne shell.

Appendix C, "The C Shell," describes shell programming with the C shell.

Appendix D, "The Korn Shell," describes shell programming with the Korn shell.

Appendix E, "The awk/nawk Programming Language," shows you how to program with **awk** and **nawk** (new **awk**).

Because so many UNIX commands have esoteric names, command *functions*, not command *names*, are arranged alphabetically within each chapter. If you want to search a file for text, you should find it easier to look up "Search for text in a file" than "**grep**." However, if you know the name of the command you want, you'll find it listed in the Command Index at the end of the book.

The intent of the publisher is to keep this book to a moderate length and to provide a reference for users who are new to the UNIX system.

Conventions

This book uses the following typesetting conventions to convey information:

Commands and options that you type literally are printed in **bold** (for example, **ls -l**). Names of directories and files are also **bold** (for example, **/usr/mktg/news**).

Generic terms for which you are to substitute an actual name are printed in *italic* (for example, *file*). When you see *file*, type the name of a file.

Optional items on a command line are enclosed in brackets (for example, [**-s**]). Here, you have the option of typing or not typing **-s**.

The options for some commands may be shown in *bundled* form (for example, [**-abdek**]). This tells you two facts: (1) You can use any of the optional letters shown; (2) you can bundle two or more of them (for example, **-ad** instead of **-a -d** or **-bek** instead of **-b -e -k**).

Most sections close with cross-references to related sections (**See Also**). If the related command is in another chapter, the chapter number is shown; if the command is in the same chapter, the chapter reference is omitted.

1

UNIX Concepts

This chapter discusses some of the basic concepts that underlie the UNIX system. This information will be presented once in this chapter, rather than repeated many times in the chapters that cover specific commands.

UNIX System V, like other operating systems, relies on the concept of a *file*, which is described in the next section. It also relies on the concept of a *process*, which is described at the end of this chapter.

Files and Directories

On a computer, a *file* is a collection of characters that is stored electronically. Letters, memos, databases, accounting records, application programs, and even the components of the operating system itself are all stored as files. The most common storage medium today is the magnetic *disk*.

Hierarchical Directory System of UNIX

Because so many files are stored on one computer, there must be a systematic method for organizing them. In the UNIX system, that method is called a *file system*. A file system is a structured collection of *directories* containing files. A directory is a file that is designated as a storage location for other files.

In the UNIX system, directories are arranged in a hierarchical order, with a single *root directory* (or *root*) at the top. A limited number of primary directories are stored in the root; each primary directory, in turn, contains its own subdirectories; and so on. The directory in which any given directory resides is called the *parent directory* (or *parent*), denoted by two periods (..). The root directory, denoted by a slash (/), is the only directory in a UNIX file system that is its own parent.

When you log into a UNIX system, you are switched to a directory that has been assigned to you. This is called your *home directory*, sometimes denoted by its environmental variable name, $HOME. You can create subdirectories in your home directory to organize your own files.

Although directory names and locations may vary from system to system, certain directories are the same on every UNIX system all over the world. For example, device files are always stored in directory /**dev**, binary files (or executable program files) in /**bin**, temporary files in /**tmp**, and system administration files in /**etc**. Home directories for users are generally stored in a directory called /**usr**; however, the name can vary from system to system (/**usr1**, /**usr2**, /**u1**, /**u2**, and so on). Appendix A, "The UNIX Locator," provides the location of many of the most commonly used files and directories.

File Permissions

One way to prevent users from accessing unauthorized files and directories on a UNIX system is a system of file-access permissions. The various permissions granted or denied for a particular file are part of its *file mode*.

Each file is assigned one permission with respect to reading, one for writing, and one for execution. These determine who is allowed to read the file, write to the file, and execute the file (if it's a command). The permissions apply, in turn, to the owner of the file, members of the owner's working group, and all other users on the system. All together, each file has nine permissions: three for the owner, three for the owner's group, and three for others.

The notation used for permissions is as follows:

r	Permission to read
w	Permission to write
x	Permission to execute
-	Permission denied for any of the above

The three basic permissions are interpreted in a slightly different way for directories than they are for ordinary files. The differences are shown in Table 1-1.

The command line **ls -l** displays permissions assigned to files in a directory, along with other information. One item in one column of output from the **ls -l** command may look like this:

```
rwxrwxrwx
```

Table 1-1 File Permissions Versus Directory Permissions

	Ordinary File	*Directory*
Read	Look at the contents of the file	Display the names of files in the directory
Write	Change the contents of the file	Add files to, or remove files from, the directory
Execute	Treat the file as a UNIX command	Change to the directory, search it, copy files from it

This means that read, write, and execute permissions have been granted to the owner (rwx), the group owner (rwx), and all other users (rwx). For those familiar with binary and octal numbers, the symbolic representation of the permissions (rwx rwx rwx) can be translated into binary form (111 111 111), which is equivalent to the octal number 777. System administrators usually use octal notation. As another example, rw- rw- r-- translates to 110 110 100, which is 664.

The Shell

The *shell* is the command interpreter. It prompts you for input, reads your input, interprets it, and then either executes it or displays an error message. If it executes it, it either displays the output on your screen or stores it in a file, depending on what you requested.

So far, we've talked about "the" shell. Unfortunately for the new user, there's more than one. The original shell from the 1960s is called the *Bourne shell*, after its author. A second shell that was developed at Berkeley during the 1970s is called the *C shell*, after the C language. A third shell that originated at AT&T during the 1980s is called the *Korn shell*, after its author. The Korn shell is a superset of the Bourne shell, with many features of the C shell. The Korn shell is the standard shell for System V, Release 4. However, your system may have more than one shell available.

The shell presents you with a prompt on the screen, called the *shell prompt*. What this prompt looks like depends on what kind of shell you have (or what level of user you are). Here are some possibilities:

$	Bourne shell prompt
%	Standard C shell prompt
$	Standard Korn shell prompt
#	System administrator's prompt

3

If you have either the C shell or the Korn shell, you can design your own custom prompt. The most popular custom-designed prompt features automatic numbering of your command lines. The idea is that you can refer to these line numbers in subsequent command lines. With one of these, your prompt could look like this:

```
[23]    Custom designed shell prompt (C or Korn)
```

In the blank space after this prompt, you type a *command line*. A command line must contain at least a command. It may also contain an *option*, several options, a filename, several filenames, or a combination of these items. After you've typed a command line, you may see something as simple as this:

```
$ date_
```

or as involved as this:

```
$ mv -i task.1 value.b invoice.mar /usr/eng/prod/new_
```

In these examples, the **bold** text indicates what you've typed and the underscore (_) indicates the cursor. In later chapters, the shell prompt and the cursor are omitted.

Command-Line Entries

To execute the command line, press the **Return** (or **Enter**) key. In later chapters, the words "Enter the command line" mean, "Type the command line after the shell prompt and press **Return**." However, neither the shell prompt nor the **Return** key will be shown in most command-line examples.

Options

The options for a UNIX command that enable you to modify its operation vary from one command to another. Most options are denoted by a minus sign (-) followed by a letter of the alphabet. Some options stand alone; others are coupled with a number or a string of text. Occasionally, an option is denoted by a plus sign (+) followed by a letter or a number.

If a command has more than one option, you can always enter them separately on the command line. In most instances, you can also *bundle* them; that is, you can group the letters together behind a single minus sign. For example, the command line

```
$ cat -v -e -t page
```

is equivalent to the bundled option version:

```
$ cat -vet page
```

Arguments

Some commands also have *arguments*. The most common argument is a filename, or a list of filenames. Other arguments include a pattern to be matched; a variable with an assigned value; or a hyphen (-), which indicates reading from the standard input instead of from a file.

Redirection

In the absence of other instructions, you generally provide input via your keyboard and receive output on your video screen. However, you can *redirect* input and output. You can redirect input from a file instead of your keyboard and you can redirect output to a file, a printer, another terminal, or another device (such as a tape or diskette drive).

Three symbols are used for redirection:

<   Redirect input from
>   Redirect output to
>>   Redirect output and append to

To redirect the output of the **cat** command to another file called **save**, you would use a command line like this:

```
$ cat > save
```

The effect of this command line is to write everything you type at your keyboard directly to file **save**.

To redirect the input of the **mail** command from the file **memo**, you would use a command line like this:

```
$ mail eve < memo
```

The effect of this command line is to send the text in file **memo** to user **eve** via electronic mail.

Pipes

UNIX commands are modular. Each one is designed to perform one task. The idea behind this singularity is that you can perform more complex tasks by combining them on a command line. The tool for accomplishing this is the **pipe**, which is denoted by a vertical bar (|). In a pipe, the output of the command on the left becomes the input of the command on the right.

For example, the **cat** command displays the contents of a file; the **page** command places text on your video monitor one screenful at a time. Suppose you have a long file called **verbose**. One way to examine **verbose** with ease is to use the following command line:

```
$ cat verbose | page
```

The effect of this command is to pipe **verbose** to the **page** command, which displays the text one screenful at a time.

As another example, suppose you want to see a list of all users logged into your UNIX system in alphabetical order. All you have to do is pipe **who** to **sort**:

```
$ who | sort
```

The effect of this command is to collect a list of the names of users logged into the system with **who**, then sort the list with **sort**.

Certain commands like **sort** can take input from one command and then pass their own output to another command. Such commands are called *filter commands* (or *filters*).

Matching Characters by Using Metacharacters

To select sets of files, you can use *wildcard* characters to reduce the amount of typing required. Characters like these are also called *metacharacters*. The notation is as follows:

.	Match a single character
*	Match any number of characters
[*list*]	Match a set of characters

For example, to display three files called **news_1**, **news_2**, and **news_3**, you can use the following command line:

```
$ cat news_.
```

To delete three files called **backup.monday**, **backup.tuesday**, and **backup.wednesday**, you can use the following:

```
$ rm backup.*
```

To move files **notes.3**, **notes.7**, and **notes.9** to a directory called **safe**, you can use the following:

```
$ mv notes.[379] ../safe
```

Commands like **grep** that search for text in files use some additional metacharacters to form *regular expressions*. These characters are as follows:

^expr	Match *expr* at beginning of line
expr$	Match *expr* at end of line
expr_1	*expr_2*	Match *expr_1* or *expr_2*
[*c-d*]	Match any character in the range given
[*^list*]	Match any character not listed
c	Escape character *c*: interpret the character literally, not as a metacharacter.

For example, to search for the word *start* at the beginning of a line, enter the following regular expression: "^start".

To search for the word *stop* at the end of a line, enter the following: "stop$".

To search for a blank line, enter the following: "^$".

Metacharacters are used in the following commands:

> Edit stream of text (**sed**, Chapter 4)
> Find text in files (**grep**, **egrep**, Chapter 4)
> Screen editor (**vi**, Chapter 5)

Turning Off Special Meanings of Metacharacters

If you want the shell to interpret a metacharacter literally, you can turn off its special meaning—that is, tell UNIX to treat it as a literal character—by preceding it with a backslash. For example, * means an asterisk character, not the wildcard that denotes any character. Turning off the special meaning of a metacharacter is referred to as *escaping* the character.

Commands and Processes

A *command* is a request for processing that you enter on the command line. Once the shell interprets your entry, it spawns a *process* that works in the computer's memory. The program that interacts directly with the system hardware, called the *kernel*, assigns a *process identification number (PID)* to each process.

A process that interacts with you during processing is called a *foreground process*. On a UNIX system, you can also initiate a number of *background processes*, which work on their own without interacting with you. By enabling you to run several background processes, along with one foreground process, simultaneously, the UNIX system offers you *multitasking* capability. It is as if you had more than one computer at your disposal.

The procedure for running a background process is to append an ampersand character (&) at the end of your command line. For example, to remove files called **trash.mon**, **trash.tue**, and so on, in the background, use the following command line:

```
$ rm trash.* &
```

Because so many processes can be active on a system at one time, there must be an orderly way of allocating to each process the time and resources it needs. To begin with, the kernel assigns each process its own PID. The purpose of the PID is to uniquely identify each process on the system. The numbers start at 0 and go as high as 32,767. Process 0 is the scheduler (**sched**); process 1 is the initialization process (**init**); next come three administrative processes, 2, 3, and 4 (**pageout**, **fsflush**, and **kmdaemon**), which handle processes for users, disk input/output (I/O), and processes for the operating system.

Background processes that run automatically are called *daemon processes*, or *daemons*. These processes usually handle tasks that must be carried at given time intervals or when there is a demand. One daemon, called **cron,** takes care of executing commands that are preset to be run at specified times on specified days. Another one, called **lpsched**, makes sure that files queued for printing reach the printer. The system processes **pageout, kmdaemon**, and **fsflush** are also daemons.

The **init** process spawns the login shell for each user who logs into the system. Then the login shell spawns each process the user requests. These user-initiated processes, in turn, may spawn other processes. The result is a hierarchical *tree* of processes, similar to the one for files and directories. The process that spawns another is called the *parent*, while the process spawned is called the *child*.

A process like a login shell generates an entire family of processes. Each new process beginning is said to be *born*; each process that terminates is said to *die*. (If you terminate a process before completion, the process is said to be *killed*.) The family of processes generated is called a *process group*, or *session*. The patriarchal process is called a *process group leader*, or *session leader*.

Many generations of processes may be active at any one moment on a UNIX system, each with its own process ID (PID) and priority. The lower the PID, the earlier the process was spawned. Some processes have short lives on the system; others run as long as the system runs. Only the super-user can increase the priority of a process. However, any user can decrease the priority of a process by using a command called **nice**. Just insert **nice** in front of the command name on the command line. Ordinarily, when you log out, all processes in the session are killed. To allow a process to keep running after you log out, use the **nohup** command. The command that enables you to terminate a process that is out of control or taking too long to execute is **kill**.

Starting with UNIX System V, Release 4, there are three *priority classes*: *system (SYS) class*, *real-time (RT) class*, and *time-sharing (TS) class*. System class is reserved for use by the kernel; real-time class includes processes that require immediate attention and preempt all processes in time-sharing class; time-sharing class includes all ordinary processes. Within time-sharing class, each process has its own priority, which can be lowered with the **nice** command.

The UNIX system is a collection of files, which store information on disk, and processes, which carry out tasks in memory and interact with all the computer's devices. A command is stored as a file, but when activated, a command becomes a process. The chapters that follow deal with UNIX commands.

2

General-Purpose Utilities

This chapter describes the commands that provide the most basic services. Most of them relate to the system as a whole, processes, or directories.

Change Directory

```
$   cd [path]
$   cd ~[[user/]subdirectory]
$   cd previous next
```

Use **cd** to switch to another directory. There are several ways to indicate the desired directory.

Application   To return to your home directory ($HOME), enter **cd** without an argument.

To change to a subdirectory of your current directory, enter the name as the argument. For example, to change to subdirectory **plans** in the current directory, enter **cd plans**.

To change to a directory outside your current directory, enter its full pathname as the argument. For example, to change to directory **/usr/mktg/plans**, enter **cd /usr/mktg/plans**. If your current directory and the target directory have the same parent directory, you can use the parent (..) notation in the argument. For example, to change from **/usr/mktg/log** to **/usr/mktg/plans**, you can enter **cd ../plans**.

To change to a subdirectory in your home directory, use a tilde (~), followed by the name of the subdirectory. For example, to move to subdirectory **/sched/1994** in your home directory, enter **cd ~/sched/1994**.

To change to a subdirectory in another user's home directory, use a tilde (~), followed by the user's login name, followed by the name of the subdirectory. For example, to move to directory **/sched/1994** in the home directory of user skeeter, enter **cd ~skeeter/sched/1994**.

Suppose you have a group of directories that contain similar or identical subdirectory names (such as **/usr/mktg/inv/test/new**, **/usr/mktg/stu/test/new**, and **/usr/mktg/real/test/new**). To change from one of these directories to another, you can have the shell change the part of the name that differs without having to enter the entire pathname each time. For example, if you are working in **/usr/mktg/inv/test/new** and you want to change to **/usr/mktg/real/test/new**, you can enter the command **cd inv real**. The shell will replace **inv** with **real** in your pathname and move you to the new directory.

Note   If the target directory does not exist or if you don't have execute permission for the directory, an error message will result. You can assign to the **CDPATH** environmental variable a list of directory names for **cd** to check. Place this assignment in either **.profile** (Bourne or Korn shell) or **.login** (C shell).

See Also   Display name of directory (**pwd**)

```
/usr/nelson> cat .profile
:
PATH=/usr/ucb:/usr/bin:/usr/local/bin:$HOME/bin:.
TERM=vt100
MAIL=/usr/spool/mail/`logname`              # mailbox location
VISUAL=/usr/ucb/vi
MAILCHECK=8
export MAILCHECK VISUAL PATH TERM
stty erase
HOST=`hostname`
umask 022                                   # set file creation mask
#
#       EDITOR OPTIONS
#       Default editor is vi.
#       VISUAL=/usr/ucb/vi

#       To make emacs the default editor, remove comment from next line
#       VISUAL=/usr/local/bin/emacs

PS1='$HOST:$PWD> '
export PATH MAIL VISUAL
```

An example of a .profile file

Change Group

```
$ newgrp [-] [group]
```

Use **newgrp** to change to a new working group.

Application To change to group **acctg**, enter **newgrp acctg**. If the new group exists and you have access to it, the command will be executed and your group ID will be changed.

To change from another group back to your login group, enter **newgrp** without an argument.

Options - Change to the new environment as if you had logged out and logged in again as a member of the new group

group New group you are joining

Note Although you can belong to more than one group, the system acknowledges only one at a time. If you belong to more than one, use this command to switch from one to another. Use **id** to display your current user and group IDs.

See Also Display files in a directory (**ls**)
Change group (**chgrp**, Chapter 8)
Create environment (**env**, Chapter 8)

Change Password

```
$ passwd [-s]
```

Use **passwd** to change your password; show password attributes.

Application To change your password, enter the command **passwd** by itself.

Option **-s** Show password attributes. The attributes will be displayed as follows:

user status [mm/dd/yy min max notice]

user Your user name, or login name
status One of three codes:

NP no password
PS password
LK locked

mm/dd/yy Date when you last changed your password
min Minimum number of days required before you can change your password

max	Maximum number of days allowed before you have to change your password (the number of days before your password expires)
notice	Number of days notice you are given before your password expires

The first two attributes (*user_ID*, *status*) are always displayed; the last four (*mm/dd/yy*, *min*, *max*, *notice*) are displayed only if your system administrator has implemented password aging on your UNIX system.

Note   Computers, especially multiuser computers, attract mischief-makers. User passwords afford your system some measure of protection, particularly if they are long enough and clever enough to thwart unauthorized entries.

To be acceptable, your password must contain at least six characters, two of which must be alphabetic and one of which must be either a number or a special character. You can use a longer password, but only the first eight characters are significant. Your password cannot be a rearrangement of your login name.

It is up to your system administrator to require users to have passwords. In addition, your system administrator can also implement and enforce password aging, which forces users to change passwords periodically.

A system administrator can use **passwd** to change any user's password. The **passwd** command is revisited in Chapter 8.

See Also   Log into system (**login**)
Change password (**passwd**, Chapter 8)
Substitute user (**su**, Chapter 8)

Check Process Status

```
$ ps [-acdefjl][-g list][-p list][-s list][-t list][-u list]
```

Use **ps** to report the status of a process, or a set of processes, including at least four items of information about each process: the process ID assigned by the system, the control terminal, the amount of time the process has been executing, and the name of the command being executed.

Various options enable you to display ten additional items of information and specify which processes to report on.

Application   To display the most basic information about processes active on your system, enter the command **ps** by itself. The four items of information will be listed under the following column headings: PID, TTY, TIME, COMMAND.

Options   To display additional information or to limit the report to a specific set of processes, use one or more of the following options:

-a   Show all processes except group leaders and those not controlled by a terminal

-c   Show information about scheduler priorities

-d   Show all processes except group leaders

-e   Show all active processes

-f   Show a full listing, which includes the user ID of the originator of the process, the process ID of the parent process, the time at which the process started, and processor use. The eight column headings are as follows: UID, PID, PPID, C, STIME, TTY, TIME, COMMAND

-j   Show session and process group IDs

-l   Show a long listing, which includes with the full listing the flags for the process, the status of the process, the priority of the process, the "nice" value that determines the priority, the memory address of the process, the size of the process in blocks, and the address of any event for which the process may be waiting. The column headings are as follows: F, S, UID, PID, PPID, C, PRI, NI, ADDR, SZ, WCHAN, TTY, TIME, COMMAND

-g *list*   Show only processes whose group leaders are listed

-p *list*   Show only processes whose process IDs are listed

-s *list* Show information about session leaders listed
-t *list* Show only processes from the terminals listed
-u *list* Show only processes whose user IDs are listed

The items in each *list* can be either separated by commas or separated by spaces and enclosed within double quotes.

Note   Because you can see what your foreground process is doing, you generally use the **ps** command to follow the progress of your background processes. The information reported is constantly changing as the system swaps processes in and out of memory. Chapter 8 describes the more sophisticated and technical uses of **ps**.

See Also   Terminate a process (**kill**)
Set processing priorities (**nice**, Chapter 8)
Check process status (**ps**, Chapter 8)

```
/usr/nelson> ps
  PID TT STAT   TIME COMMAND
15484 sb S     0:00 -ksh (ksh)
15716 sb R     0:00 ps

/usr/nelson> ps -l
      F UID   PID  PPID CP PRI NI  SZ  RSS WCHAN    STAT TT   TIME COMMAND
204880012772 15484 13351  3   5  0  24  168 child    S    sb  0:00 -ksh (ksh)
200000012772 15768 15484 29  32  0 288  536          R    sb  0:00 ps -l

/usr/nelson> ps -f
ps: f: unknown option
ps: usage: ps [-acCegjklnrStuvwxU] [num] [kernel_name] [c_dump_file]
[swap_file]
```

Three examples of the ps command

Compare Directories

```
$ dircmp [-d][-s][-wn] dir_1 dir_2
```

Use **dircmp** to compare files in two directories and provide the following information: files found only in the first directory; the files found only in the second directory; and names common to both directories.

In addition, **dircmp** distinguishes pairs of common filenames as follows: those that are directories; those that have different contents; and those that have the same contents.

Application To compare two directories called **acct** and **plan**, enter **dircmp acct plan**.

Options   **-d**   Compare pairs of common files.

            -s   Suppress messages about files with the same contents.

            -w*n*   Change the width of each output line from the default (72 characters) to *n* characters.

Note   To prevent names of files common to both directories from being listed twice (once for each directory), you can filter the output of **dircmp** through **uniq**. Then each filename will be listed only once.

See Also   Compare files for differences (**diff**, Chapter 3)

Continue Processing

```
$ nohup command [option(s)] [arg(s)]
```

Use **nohup** to execute a command that cannot be interrupted by a telephone hang-up or a quit signal.

Application   To begin a spell-checking job on a long file called **mammoth** and then log out or hang up, enter **nohup spell mammoth &**.

            If you have a pipeline, be sure to include **nohup** with each segment of pipe. For example, **nohup troff -Tlaser report | nohup lp &**.

Options   *command*   The command to be executed

            option(s)   Any options required by the command

            arg(s)   Any arguments required by the command

Note   The **nohup** command enables you to start a job and log out of the system while the job runs.

Copy Session

```
$ script [-a] [file]
```

Use **script** to make a copy of a terminal session and store it in a file. By default, the file is called *typescript*.

Application   To make a copy of the current session to be stored in the file **typescript**, enter **script**. To store the output in a file called **session**, enter **script session**.

Option   -a   Append the output to the target file

Note   The **script** command works like the capture feature of many popular communications programs.

Create a Directory

```
$ mkdir [-m mode][-p] name(s)
```

Use **mkdir** to create a new directory or a group of directories; set the permission mode of the new directory, or directories; create a parent directory if necessary.

Application   To create a single directory, or a group of directories under the current directory, enter **mkdir**, followed by the name of the directory, or directories. For example, to create directories **acct** and **plan** in the current directory, enter **mkdir acct plan**.

To create directory **ltrs** under parent **/usr/sales/west** (assuming you're in another directory), enter **mkdir /usr/sales/west/ltrs**.

To create directory **ltrs** under parent **/usr/sales/east** (assuming **east** doesn't exist), enter **mkdir -p /usr/sales/east/ltrs**. Directory **ltrs** will be created, along with missing directory **east**.

For example, to create the same two subdirectories with permissions rwx rw- r-- (764), enter **mkdir -m 764 acct plan**.

Options   -m *mode*   Set the permission mode of the directory, or directories

-p   Create the parents of the directory or directories first

Note   In the absence of a **umask** setting, your default permission mode is 777 (rwx rwx rwx). A **umask** setting in your own initialization file or in your system's initialization file will produce a different default.

See Also   Delete a directory (**rmdir**)
Set default permissions (**umask**, Chapter 8)

Delete a Directory

```
$ rmdir [-p][-s] name(s)
```

Use **rmdir** to remove a directory or a set of directories.

Application To remove a single directory or a set of directories, enter the command, followed by the desired directory name(s). For example, to remove subdirectories **acct** and **plan** (assuming they are empty) from the current directory, enter **rmdir acct plan**.

Suppose **acct** and **plan** are the only remaining directories (or files) in parent directory **sales**. To remove all three directories, enter **rmdir -p acct plan**.

If the target directories still contain files, you must remove the files first. First enter **rm acct/*** and **rm plan/***, then **rmdir acct plan**. (For additional safety, begin with **rm -i acct/*** and **rm -i plan/***; you will thus be able to confirm the files one by one.)

Options -p Remove the parent directory of each directory deleted (provided it is empty)

-s Suppress messages generated by **-p**.
If you want to remove parent directories and suppress messages, you can bundle the two options (**-ps**).

Notes You aren't allowed to remove the current directory or its parent. You must move to another directory first, using **cd**.

You aren't allowed to remove a directory that still contains files, including subdirectories. You must remove the files first.

See Also Delete files (**rm**, Chapter 3)
Create a directory (**mkdir**)
Set default permissions (**umask**, Chapter 8)

Display a Calendar

```
$ cal [[month]year]
```

Use **cal** to display a calendar of the current month of the current year; display the calendar for any year from 1 A.D. to 9999 A.D.; display the calendar for any month of any year allowed.

Display a Calendar

Application   To display the current month, enter **cal** without any arguments.

To display a given year, enter **cal** and the number of the year. For example, to display 1995, enter **cal 1995**.

To display a month other than the current month, enter **cal**, a number representing the month (1–12), and the year. For example, to display March 1994, enter **cal 3 1994**.

Options   *month*   Month of the year in numeric form (1–12)
year   Year entered in full

Notes   Both arguments are optional. If you choose to use arguments, note the following:

Use a number to indicate the desired month: 1 (Jan), 2 (Feb), 3 (Mar), and so on, through 12 (Dec).

To identify a year, you must enter the full number, such as 1993. If you enter only 93, **cal** will interpret this as the year 93 A.D. in the first century.

See Also   Set up a reminder service (**calendar**)
Display date and time

```
/usr/nelson> cal 3 1994
      March 1994
 S  M Tu  W Th  F  S
          1  2  3  4  5
 6  7  8  9 10 11 12
13 14 15 16 17 18 19
20 21 22 23 24 25 26
27 28 29 30 31
```

Using the cal command to display a month

```
/usr/nelson> cal 1995

                              1995

        Jan                     Feb                     Mar
 S  M Tu  W Th  F  S     S  M Tu  W Th  F  S     S  M Tu  W Th  F  S
 1  2  3  4  5  6  7              1  2  3  4              1  2  3  4
 8  9 10 11 12 13 14     5  6  7  8  9 10 11     5  6  7  8  9 10 11
15 16 17 18 19 20 21    12 13 14 15 16 17 18    12 13 14 15 16 17 18
22 23 24 25 26 27 28    19 20 21 22 23 24 25    19 20 21 22 23 24 25
29 30 31                26 27 28                26 27 28 29 30 31

        Apr                     May                     Jun
 S  M Tu  W Th  F  S     S  M Tu  W Th  F  S     S  M Tu  W Th  F  S
                   1        1  2  3  4  5  6              1  2  3
 2  3  4  5  6  7  8     7  8  9 10 11 12 13     4  5  6  7  8  9 10
 9 10 11 12 13 14 15    14 15 16 17 18 19 20    11 12 13 14 15 16 17
16 17 18 19 20 21 22    21 22 23 24 25 26 27    18 19 20 21 22 23 24
23 24 25 26 27 28 29    28 29 30 31             25 26 27 28 29 30
30
        Jul                     Aug                     Sep
 S  M Tu  W Th  F  S     S  M Tu  W Th  F  S     S  M Tu  W Th  F  S
                   1        1  2  3  4  5                       1  2
 2  3  4  5  6  7  8     6  7  8  9 10 11 12     3  4  5  6  7  8  9
```

Using the cal command to display a year

Display Characters on the Screen

`$ echo [-n] [argument]`

Use **echo** to display characters or values on the screen. The characters don't have to represent text; they can be control characters. If the argument is a variable, you can display its value on the screen.

Application To display "Good morning" on your screen, enter **echo "Good morning"**.

To generate "Terminal type: [beep] *type*", enter **echo "Terminal type: \007 $TERM"**. Your terminal will beep, then display its type (for example, vt100, wyse50, or tvi950).

To leave space on the same line for a keyboard response to a prompt (Enter name:), enter **echo -n "Enter name: "**.

Option **-n** Do **not** end with a newline
Control Characters
\b Backspace
\c No newline
\f Formfeed
\n Newline
\r Carriage return
\t Tab
\v Vertical tab
\\ Backslash
\0*n* ASCII code of any character

Note You can also provide terminal control by including the **tput** command as an argument. For example, to home the cursor, you can include **tput home** as an argument.

Display Date and Time

`$ date [-u][+string]`

Use **date** to display the day of the week, the current date, and the time for your time zone (accurate to the millisecond); display the date and time in Greenwich Mean Time (GMT); and display the date and time in a format that you specify.

Display Date and Time

Application To display the date and time in the default format, enter date.

Options

-u   Display the date and time in Greenwich Mean Time (GMT)

+*str*   Specify the format for the output, using any combination of the following symbols. If the resulting string includes any spaces, enclose the string in double quotes (")

%D   Date in *mm/dd/yy* format

%j   Julian date (001–365)

%A   Day of week spelled out (Sunday, Monday, Tuesday, . . .)

%a   Day of week abbreviated (Sun, Mon, Tue, . . .)

%w   Day of week as a number (0 for Sun, 1 for Mon, 2 for Tue, . . .)

%U   Week number (00–51), starting each week with Sunday

%W   Week number (00–51), starting each week with Monday

%B   Month spelled out (January, February, March, . . .)

%b   Month abbreviated (Jan, Feb, Mar, . . .)

%h   Month abbreviated (Jan, Feb, Mar, . . .)

%m   Month as a number (01 for Jan, 02 for Feb, 03 for Mar, . . .)

%d   Day of month, always two digits (01–31)

%e   Day of month (1–31)

%y   Year in two digits, century implied (93)

%Y   Year in four digits (1993)

%T   Time in *hh:mm:ss* format

%p   Time of day indicator (AM or PM)

%   Time in *hh:mm:ss* AM/PM format

%H   Hours in military time (00–24)

%I   Hours in civilian time (11–12)

%M   Minutes (00–59)

%S   Seconds (00–59)

%Z   Name of time zone

%c   Date and time in format for a particular country

%X   Date only in format for a particular country

%x   Time only in format for a particular country

%n   Insert a newline

%t   Insert a tab

For example, to rearrange the elements of the standard display as shown, enter the following command line:

```
$ date +"%A, %B %e, %Y  %T %Z"
Friday, September 12, 1995  13:47:28 PST
$
```

Note   The preceding describes the use of **date** by any user. A system administrator can also use this command to set the date and time (see Chapter 8, "System Administration").

See Also   Set date and time (**date**, Chapter 8)

```
/usr/nelson> date
Thu May 21 20:28:49 PDT 1992

/usr/nelson> date +"%a, %h %d, %y  %t   "
Thu, May 21, 92

/usr/nelson> date +"%a, %h %d, %y  %T"
Thu, May 21, 92  20:35:41

/usr/nelson> date %j
usage: date [-a sss.fff] [-u] [+format] [yymmddhhmm[.ss]]
```

Four examples of the date command

Display Files in a Directory

```
$ ls [-1abcCdfFgilLmnopqrRstux] [file(s)] [dir(s)]
```

Use **ls** (list) to display the contents of a directory. You can display a wide variety of information about the individual files and subdirectories. The command has over 20 options.

Application   To list only the names of files and subdirectories in the current directory, enter **ls**. For another directory, say **totals** under the same parent, enter **ls ../totals**. To see the names of files **acct.100**, **acct.101**, **acct.102**,... , enter **ls acct.* ../totals**.

To display filenames for the current directory in columns, sorted down, enter **ls -C**.

To indicate which files in the current directory are not ordinary files, enter **ls -F**. Each directory name will be followed by a slash (/), the name of each executable file will be followed by an asterisk (*), and the name of each symbolic link will be followed by an at sign (@).

To obtain a long listing, use the -l option. The result will be a full line of information for each file, including file type, modes, number of links, owner, group, date and time of last modification, and name. Here is an example:

```
-rwxrw-r--  3  larry  eng  12 Mar 93 11:43  memo
```

In this example, the first character (-) indicates that this is an ordinary file. Other possible characters that may be used are as follows:

d Directory
c Character special file
b Block special file
p Named pipe (FIFO)

The next nine characters (rwxrw-r--) indicate the file-access permissions (or mode) assigned to the file. These characters are explained in Chapter 1.

Options

-1 Display one item per line (one-column format)

-a Display all filenames, even those that begin with a period (.)

-b Display invisible characters in octal

-c Display in order of last modification of file information

-C Display in multiple columns with entries sorted down

-d For directories, display name only—not contents

-f Treat each argument as a directory (the current directory is the default); display contents in order of file creation

-F Display / after directory names, * after names of executable files, and @ after names of symbolic links

-g Same as -l (long), but omit owner

-i Precede each filename with its i-node number

-l Long format: Display a line of information about each file, including: modes, number of links, owner, group, size, time of last modification, and filename; for special files, replace the size with major and minor numbers

-L If the name is a symbolic link, list the true file or directory name

-m Display names across the screen, separated by commas

-n   Same as long (-l), but replace owner and group
     names with owner and group numbers
-o   Same as long (-l), but omit group
-p   Display / after the name of each directory
-q   Display ? to represent each invisible character
-r   Sort in reverse order
-R   Recursively list subdirectories
-s   Display each size in blocks instead of bytes
-t   Sort by modification time
-u   With -t or -l, replace time of last modification with
     time of last access
-x   Display in multicolumn format, sorted across

Note   The ls command, which corresponds to the DOS dir
           command, is one of the most useful and most commonly
           used.

See Also   Change file-access permissions (chmod, Chapter 3)
               Change file ownership (chown, Chapter 8)
               Change group (chgrp, Chapter 8)
               Find a file (find, Chapter 3)
               Link a file (ln, Chapter 3)
               Move or rename a file (mv, Chapter 3)
               Delete files (rm, Chapter 3)

```
/usr/nelson> ls
new     entry  text   test

/usr/nelson> ls -l
total 4
druxr-xr-x  2 nelson        512 May 21 20:24 entry
druxr-xr-x  2 nelson        512 May 21 20:24 new
druxr-xr-x  2 nelson        512 May 21 20:24 test
druxr-xr-x  2 nelson        512 May 21 20:24 text

/usr/nelson> ls -F
entry/  new/   test/   text/

/usr/nelson> ls -R
entry  new    test   text

entry:
region    sales      western

new:

test:

text:
```

Four examples of the ls command

Display Groups

```
$ groups [user(s)]
```

Use **groups** to display the groups to which any user, or set of users, belongs.

Application   To display the name of your own group, enter **groups**. To display the names of the groups that users **bill** and **ted** belong to, enter **groups bill ted**.

See Also   Change group (**newgrp**)
Change group (**chgrp**)

Display Large Letters

```
$ banner char(s)
```

Use **banner** to display large letters. Each line of letters occupies one-third of the screen.

Application   To display "Hello" on your screen in large letters, enter **banner Hello**. Another example: **banner "Mtg @ 3:00"** (the maximum number of characters—10).

To print BREATHE IN / PUFF NOT on a page in large letters, enter **banner "BREATHE IN" "PUFF NOT" | lp**. Each quoted expression will fill a separate line (use "" for a blank line).

To display MEET ME / DOWNSTAIRS / AT 3:00 on another user's terminal (say, tty06), enter **banner "MEET ME" "DOWNSTAIRS" "AT 3:00" > /dev/tty06**. Use this only for an emergency, because it will disrupt output on the other user's screen.

Note   You can use the **banner** command to produce large-letter signs and notices.

Display Name of Directory

```
$ pwd
```

Use **pwd** to display the full pathname of the current directory.

Application   Enter the **pwd** command; it has no arguments.

Note   Because you don't see the name of the current directory displayed on most UNIX systems, you need the **pwd** command to determine the path to that directory.

See Also   Change directory (**cd**)

Display Names of Users

```
$ listusers [-g group(s)] [-1 login(s)]
```

Use **listusers** to display a list of user names and IDs.

Application   To display names and IDs for all users, enter **listusers**. To restrict the list to those users that belong to groups **plans** and **design**, enter **listusers -g plans,design**.

Options   -g *group(s)*   Only users who belong to the group(s) named
-l *login(s)*   Only users with the login name(s) shown

For more than one group or login, separate the names with commas.

Display News

```
$ news [-ans] [item(s)]
```

Use **news** to display news items about your system.

Application   To display only the most recent items, enter **news**. To display the number of recent items, enter **news -s**. To display the names of recent items, enter **enter -n**.

Options   -a Display all items, not just the most recent
-n Display names of recent items, not contents
-s Display the number of recent items, not contents

Note   The **news** command keeps track of the last time you checked the news; then, the next time you invoke the command, you see only items more recent (unless you use **-a**).

Display System Name

```
$ uname [-amnprsv]
```

Use **uname** to display the name of your UNIX system (default information); optionally, display the network node name, the UNIX version and release number, the processor type, and the hardware name.

Application   To display the name of your UNIX system, enter the **uname** command without an argument (or with the **-s** option).

To display the name of the network node for your system, enter **uname -n**.

To display the version and release number of your UNIX system, enter **uname -vr.**

Options   -n   Display the name of your system's network node
-v   Display the version of your UNIX system
-r   Display the release number of your UNIX system
-p   Display the type of processor used by your computer
-m   Display the model number of your computer
-a   Display all of the above information at once

Note   With more and more systems connected to one another on networks, it can be useful to find out the name of the system which you are currently logged into. A system administrator can also use the command to change the name of a system (Chapter 8).

See Also   Change system name (**uname**, Chapter 8)

Display Terminal Name

```
$ tty [-ls]
```

Use **tty** to display the name of your terminal.

Application   To display the name of your terminal (assumed to be an asynchronous device), enter the **tty** command without an argument.

Options   -l   Display the line number of your terminal (provided it is a synchronous device)

-s   Silent mode: Return only an exit status code without
     displaying a name:

    0   Standard input device is a terminal
    2   Invalid options were entered
    1   Neither 0 nor 2

Note   You may want to use this command just to find out the
name of your terminal's port on the system. You may
also want to see the new port number after moving your
terminal. Finally, you may want to use **tty -l** in a shell
script to test the exit status code.

Display Terminal Settings

$ stty [-ag] *options*

Use **stty** to display operational settings for your terminal.

Application   To display your terminal's basic operational settings,
enter **stty** without an argument. For a complete display,
enter **stty -a**.

To notify the system of a change in the operation of your
terminal, you can enter one or more of a set of over 70
options. For example, to indicate a change in the speed
of your terminal to 2400 bit/s, you can enter **stty 2400**.

If your terminal's settings are set incorrectly and your
terminal is behaving strangely as a result, you can
remedy the problem by entering **stty sane**. This will
produce a combination of settings that should work for
most terminals.

The simplest and most common terminal modes are
listed in this section. A more complete list is found under
stty in Chapter 8.

Options   -a   All: display all terminal settings
    -g   Display settings in a format suitable for use as an
        argument for the **stty** command

Terminal modes
The most common terminal modes are as follows:

cs*n*   Character size: use *n* bits per character (5–8)
line = *n*   Line discipline: set to *n* (0–127)

char *c*		Set one of the following control characters:
	eof	End of file (default **Ctrl D**)
	erase	Erase character [on left] (default **#**)
	intr	Interrupt signal [to stop a process] (default **Del**)
	kill	Kill character [to erase the command line] (default **@**)
	quit	Quit signal [to create a core image file] (default **Ctrl L**)
	swtch	Switch character [to switch to a shell control layer] (default **Ctrl Z**)
rate		Data rate (or speed): 110, 300, 600, 1200, 1800, 2400, 4800, 9600, 19200, or 38400)
sane		Sane mode: settings that work for most terminals (even parity, modem control, character 7, and so on)
terminal		Complete settings for one of the default terminals: tty33, tty37, vt105, tn300, ti700, or tek)
ek		Set erase (**#**) and kill (**@**)

For a complete list of terminal modes, see **stty**, Chapter 8.

Note

The **stty** command does not change the operation of your terminal; it merely *informs* the system of a change. To change the way your terminal works, you have to change the terminal itself. You either have to flip DIP switches or make menu selections from a setup menu, depending on how your terminal works. Most terminals designed since the mid-1980s use setup menus; earlier models use DIP switches.

See Also

Change terminal settings (**stty**, Chapter 8)

```
/usr/nelson> stty
speed 19200 baud; evenp
erase = ^H
-inpck imaxbel -tabs
iexten crt
/usr/nelson> stty -a
speed 19200 baud, 0 rows, 0 columns
parenb -parodd cs7 -cstopb -hupcl cread -clocal -crtscts
-ignbrk brkint ignpar -parmrk -inpck istrip -inlcr -igncr icrnl -iuclc
ixon -ixany -ixoff imaxbel
isig iexten icanon -xcase echo echoe echok -echonl -noflsh -tostop
echoctl -echoprt echoke
opost -olcuc onlcr -ocrnl -onocr -onlret -ofill -ofdel -tabs
erase   kill    werase  rprnt   flush   lnext   susp    intr    quit    stop    eof
^H      ^U      ^W      ^R      ^O      ^U      ^Z/^Y   ^C      ^\      ^S/^Q   ^D

/usr/nelson> stty -g
2526:1805:1ae:8a3b:3:1c:8:15:4:0:0:0:11:13:1a:19:12:f:17:16:0
```

Two examples of the stty command

Display User Names

```
$ who [am i] [-qs]
```

Use **who** to display the names of all users currently logged onto your UNIX system; optionally, display your login name; optionally, display a variety of other information.

Application To display who is logged onto your system, enter the **who** command without an argument (or with the default **-s** option).

To display a quick listing (names only, not other information), enter **who -q**.

To display your own login name, enter **who am i**.

Options
- **am i** Display your own login name
- **-q** Display a quick listing (names of users, total number only)
- **-s** Display current user's login name, terminal line, and time logged in (default option)

Note This section covers only the most basic options. Many more options are covered in Chapter 8.

See Also Display date and time (**date**)
Log into system (**login**)
Set terminal access (**mesg**)

```
/usr/nelson> who
nedd      console Apr 27 18:58
lynn      tty00   Apr 27 17:26
brady     tty01   Apr 27 19:39
ellen     tty02   Apr 27 20:38
hank      tty03   Apr 27 20:31
lnke      tty04   Apr 27 17:39
henryt    tty05   Apr 27 20:39
mel       tty06   Apr 27 18:24
jerry     tty07   Apr 27 19:32
paulu     tty08   Apr 27 17:48
dug       tty09   Apr 27 19:41
robertu   tty0b   Apr 27 20:48
venkman   tty0c   Apr 27 16:26
carl      tty0d   Apr 27 20:00
bkaufman  tty0e   Apr 27 20:16
bobden    tty0f   Apr 27 20:47
jazlick   tty10   Apr 27 20:47
bunnyr    tty11   Apr 27 19:32
phogan    tty12   Apr 27 19:32
nedd      tty13   Apr 27 18:14
cougarz   tty14   Apr 27 20:11
kingston  tty15   Apr 27 20:48
renker    tty16   Apr 27 20:08
```

The who command

Log into System

```
$ login [user_id] [settings]
```

Use the **login** command to log into your UNIX system. You can also specify settings for environmental variables.

Application   To log into the system under a different login name, enter the **login** command without an argument. The system will then prompt you for your new login name and password. You can also include your new login name as an argument to the command.

If you want to change any of your environmental variables, you can enter them on the command line in the format *var=value*. You can also wait until after login to enter them manually. If you don't set any of them, the system will use default values.

For example, to change your terminal type to VT100 when you log in, enter **login TERM=vt100**.

Note   You can use the **login** command after you're already logged in if you need to log in under another user name.

See Also   Change password (**passwd**)
Set environmental variables (**env**, Chapter 8)
Substitute user (**su**, Chapter 8)

Redirect and Display Output

```
$ tee [-a][-i] file
```

Use **tee** to redirect output to a file while you display it on the screen. This command always receives its input from another command through a pipe.

Application   To write text to a given file and display it on the screen simultaneously, enter the pipe symbol (|), the **tee** command, and the name of the target file. If the file already exists, it will be overwritten; if it doesn't exist, it will be created.

For example, to save the sorted output of file **names** in a second file called **nsort** while you are viewing it on the screen, enter **sort names** | **tee nsort**. If you want to print the output instead of viewing it on the screen, enter **sort names** | **tee nsort** | **lp**.

To make two copies of a file called **memo** that is formatted by **pr** and also to print a copy, enter **pr memo** | **tee ../ralph policy** | **lp**. One copy of **memo**, called **ralph**, will be stored in the parent directory; another copy, called **policy**, will be stored in the current directory.

Suppose you want to call up another UNIX system and keep a record of the remote session in a file called **remote**. Then you can enter **cu -s 2400 3456000** | **tee remote**. You will be able to see all output displayed on your screen while it is being stored in **remote** for future reference.

Options   -a   Append output to the file, rather than overwrite the file
　　　　　　　-i   Ignore interrupts from the system

Note   This command enables you to view text on the screen while you are also saving it in a file. If you also want a printed copy of the text, you can pipe the output of **tee** to the printer.

Set Up a Reminder Service

```
$ calendar [-]
```

This command, along with its accompanying file, provides you with an electronic reminder service. Dates that you have to remember will be sent to you via electronic mail a day in advance.

Application   First, you need a file in your home directory that is named **calendar**. In this file you enter important appointments and events in a two-column format. For each line, the first column contains a date and the second contains a description of the event or appointment.

The date may be entered in one of the following formats:

9/17
Sep. 17
September 17

You can use spaces or tabs to separate dates from descriptions. Here is a sample **calendar** file:

```
5/6        Meet with Janice at 9:30
5/7        Lunch at Luigi's with Bernie
5/8        Presentation at MGI at 1:30
5/8        Dinner at Chez Pierre's at 5:45 (Robin)
```

Once you have your **calendar** file set up, the system reminds you automatically of any event scheduled for today or tomorrow, using electronic mail. In addition, you can call up the reminder service manually at any time by executing the **calendar** command without an argument.

To check the **calendar** file of every user on the system and mail yourself the events for today and tomorrow, enter **calendar** with the - option.

Note   The **calendar** system considers only work days, ignoring weekends. If "today" is Friday, **calendar** regards Monday as "tomorrow."

See Also   Display a calendar (**cal**)
Display date and time (**date**)
Send and receive mail (**mail**, Chapter 7)

Substitute User

```
$ su [-] [user] [-c command] [-r command]
```

Use **su** to become another user without having to log out and log back in again. Your current shell is suspended while you switch to the shell of the substitute user.

Application   To become user **jeremy**, enter **su jeremy**. A prompt will require you to enter **jeremy**'s password. To return to your own user name at the end of this session, enter **Ctrl D**.

Options   -   Change to the environment of the new user
             user   Any user name
             -c *command*   Pass *command* to the new shell and execute it
             -r *command*   Pass *command* to a restricted shell and execute it

> *command*   Any command string acceptable to the
>   target shell

Note   After working in the target user's shell, you can log out
             of it and resume work in your original shell.

See Also Log into system (**login**)
             Change password (**passwd**)

Suspend Execution

```
$ sleep [s]
```

Use **sleep** to suspend execution for the number of seconds indicated.

Application To wait one hour, then sound your terminal's beeper and
                display a message on your screen, enter **sleep 3600; echo
                "\007 Next interview in five minutes\n" &.**

Option   *s* Number of seconds to suspend execution

Note   You can use **sleep** either to defer execution of another
                command or to provide pauses in the middle of
                execution. Like **nice**, **sleep** enables you to relinquish
                processing time to other users on the system.

                60 seconds = 1 minute
                600 seconds = 10 minutes
                3600 seconds = 1 hour

See Also   Wait for completion of a process (**wait**)

Terminate a Process

```
$ kill [option] pid(s)
$ kill option pgid(s)
$ kill -1
```

Use **kill** to terminate a process or a set of processes; send a signal.

Application To terminate a background process, enter the command
                kill, followed by the desired process ID (PID), obtained
                from running the **ps** command. This sends signal
                number 15 (software termination)—the default—to the
                process, as in **kill 6723**.

If the process keeps running, enter **kill**, the **-9** option, and the same PID. This step sends signal number 9 (kill), which the process cannot ignore or catch, as in **kill -9 6723**.

To terminate all background processes in the same group, enter **kill 0** (the command followed by zero). Signals 9 and 15 are the most common. To list all signals available on your system, enter **kill** followed by the **-1** (list) option.

Notes   Use the **kill** command to terminate background processes that are looping endlessly or that have hung. A process may hang while you are attempting to interact with a nonexistent or disconnected device on the system. To terminate a foreground process, press the Del key.

See Also   Check process status (**ps**)

Wait for Completion of a Process

```
$ wait [PID]
```

Use **wait** to wait for one process, usually in the background, to complete before you run the next process.

Application   To wait for all your background processes to complete before you start the next process, enter **wait**. To wait for the completion of the process identified by process ID (PID) 12763, enter **wait 12763**.

Option   *PID*   The process ID of the process you want to wait for

Note   The **wait** command enables you to make sure one process has completed successfully before you execute another.

See Also   Suspend execution (**sleep**)

3

File Handling

This chapter describes those commands that provide basic file-handling features. These include commands that you use to copy, move, delete, display, compare, concatenate, and link files. As you create directories and fill them with files, you will use many of these basic commands on a daily basis.

As a general rule, the commands described in this chapter don't alter the contents of files. The commands that change, rearrange, and manipulate the contents of files are found in the next chapter.

Change File-Access Permissions

```
$ chmod [-R] modes file(s)
```

Use **chmod** to change file-access permissions (which are part of the file mode) for a given file or group of files. The files in question can be either ordinary files or directories.

You can enter the *modes* argument in either symbolic form or in numeric form. In this chapter, we'll discuss only the symbolic form. The numeric form is covered in Chapter 8.

Application Before you can enter modes in symbolic form, you have to know the symbols, which are as follows:

u User (the owner of the file)
g The group owner
o Others on the system
a All of the above (**ugo**)
+ Add permission to current permissions
- Remove permission from current permissions
= Set absolute permissions (remove all current permissions and set new permissions from scratch); **u**, **g**, or **o** following = means to use the current permission for the owner, group, or others
r Permission to read

w Permission to write

x Permission to execute

l Mandatory lock during file access

To set permissions, enter **chmod**, the symbolic modes, and the name of the file or files. For example, to add execute permission for yourself for file **test**, you can enter **chmod u+x test**. To remove write permission for your group, you can enter **chmod g-w test**.

To set more than one mode, separate each symbolic setting from the next with a comma (without spaces). For example, to add write permission for yourself and read permission for others, you can enter **chmod u+w,o+r test**.

To add execute permission for your group and for others, enter **chmod go+x test**. To add execute permission for yourself and remove write permission for your group and for others, enter **chmod u+x,go-w test**.

To cause file **test** to be locked while it is being accessed, enter **chmod a+l test**. Once you've done this, only one program can make changes to **test** at a time.

To clear all current permissions and give everyone read permission, you can enter **chmod a=rw**.

Option   -R   Descend recursively through directories

Notes   Execute permission for a file enables you to run a program you have written.

File locking means only one user at a time can access a file.

See Also   Display files in a directory (**ls**)
Change file ownership (**chown**, Chapter 8)
Change file-access permissions (**chmod**, Chapter 8)
Change group (**chgrp**, Chapter 8)

Check Spelling

```
$ spell [-blvx] [+local] [file(s)]
```

Use **spell** to check a file or a set of files for spelling errors. Any words that do not match the spell command's own list are displayed.

Application To check spelling in file **essay** in the current directory, enter **spell essay**.

Suppose you have a list of unusual words listed in a file called **except**, one word per line in sorted order. Then, to instruct **spell** to ignore these words, you can enter **spell +except essay**.

Suppose you have a **troff** file called **interplay**, which refers to a number of included files. To have **spell** check all files referred to, enter **spell -l interplay**.

Options
- **-b**   Check British forms of spelling
- **-l**   Check any included files referred to in the target file
- **-v**   Check derivatives and other words not literally found in **spell**'s list
- **-x**   Display possible stems of target words
- **+local**   Exclude all words listed in file *local*, which contains a sorted list of words used locally that may not be recognized in general usage

Note Compared to spelling programs that are included with most word-processing software today, **spell** is somewhat primitive. It doesn't offer alternative spellings or a facility for making corrections on the spot. You have to go back, find the errors, and correct the spelling manually (or with the aid of another command).

See Also Edit stream of text (**sed**, Chapter 4)

Compare Files Byte by Byte

```
$ cmp [-ls] file_1 file_2
```

Use **cmp** to compare two files of any type byte by byte. You can compare text files or binary files without presorting.

Application Suppose you want to compare two files called **letter** and **letter.bak**. You can do this by entering **cmp letter letter.bak**.

If the files are identical, **cmp** will return an exit code of 0 (zero) with no output; if the files are different, **cmp** will return an exit code of 1 and report the line number and byte position of the first difference encountered; if one of the files is unreadable, **cmp** will return an exit code of 2 with no output.

Options -l Display the byte position, along with the two bytes that differ, for every difference encountered (not just the first)

-s Silent mode: Return exit codes only—no output

Note Of the three commands for comparing files, **cmp** is the only one that accepts both text and nontext files, sorted and unsorted.

See Also Compare files line by line (**comm**)
Compare files for differences (**diff**)
Compare directories (**dircmp**, Chapter 2)

```
/usr/nelson/text> cat fruit.1          /usr/nelson/text> cat fruit.2
Apples have been a perennial           Apples have been a perennial
favorite with many people.             favorite with many people.
But many people prefer                 But many people choose
oranges.  Maybe it's because           oranges.  Maybe it's because
oranges are juicier, or                oranges are juicier, or
maybe it's because of their            maybe it's because of their
color.  On the other hand,             texture.  On the other hand,
there are those who swear              there are those who swear
by the sweet taste of                  by the tart taste of
cherries.  Their bright                cherries.  Their bright
red color is hard to argue             red color is hard to argue
against.                               against.

/usr/nelson/text> cmp fruit.1 fruit.2
fruit.1 fruit.2 differ: char 76, line 3
```

Comparing two files with the cmp command

Compare Files for Differences

```
$ diff [-cefhn] [-C n] [-D string] [-bitw] file_1 file_2
$ diff [-cefhn] [-S file] [-bitw] [-lrs] dir_1 dir_2
```

Use **diff** to compare two text files for differences and identify lines that need to be changed to make the two files identical. You can use **diff** with either individual text files or directories.

Application Suppose you have two files that contain the following short lists:

$ cat yard	$ cat house
1 ant	1 ant
2 bee	2 bow
3 cat	3 cat

To compare the two files for differences, enter **diff yard house**. The output will look like this:

```
2c2
< 2 bee
---
> 2 bow
```

This tells you a change (**c**) has taken place in line 2: the first file (**<**) contains "2 bee," while the second (**>**) contains "2 bow." The three hyphens (**---**) separate the contents of the two files. Other symbols used in **diff** output include addition (**a**) and deletion (**d**).

Options

-b	Ignore extra blank spaces
-c[*n*]	Show *n* lines of context for each difference (default 3)
-C[*n*]	Same as **-c**
-D *str*	Merge *file_1* with *file_2*, using C preprocessor controls
-e	Generate an **ed** script to create *file_2* from *file_1*
-f	Generate a script to create *file_2* from *file_1* (not compatible with **ed**)
-h	Fast comparison (**-e**, **-f** excluded)
-i	Ignore case
-l	Long format with pagination (directories only)
-n	Generate an **ed** script to create *file_1* from *file_2*; count the number of lines changed
-r	Recursively traverse subdirectories (directories only)
-s	List identical files (directories only)
-S *file*	Start with file *file* (directories only)
-t	Convert input tabs to output spaces
-w	Ignore spaces and tabs

Note

The output of **diff**, which isn't always easy to read, indicates text that must be appended, changed, or deleted to make the two files identical. It can also generate a script that you can use to perform the modifications required.

See Also

Compare files byte by byte (**byte**)
Compare files line by line (**comm**)

```
/usr/nelson/text> diff fruit.1 fruit.2
3c3
< But many people prefer
---
> But many people choose
7c7
< color.  On the other hand,
---
> texture.  On the other hand,
9c9
< by the sweet taste of
---
> by the tart taste of
```

Comparing two files with the diff command

Compare Files Line by Line

```
$ comm [-] [-123] file_1 file_2
```

Use the **comm** command to compare line by line text files that have been presorted.

Application The default output of **comm** consists of three columns:

Lines found   Lines found   Lines common
only in *file_1*   only in *file_2*   to both files

Options The options available with the **comm** command enable you to suppress any of these three columns:

-1 Suppress column 1 (lines found only in *file_1*)
-2 Suppress column 2 (lines found only in *file_2*)
-3 Suppress column 3 (lines common to both files)

You can bundle any two options to obtain precisely the information you are looking for.

If you use a minus sign (-), keyboard input replaces *file_1*. That is, **comm** compares your keyboard input to *file_2*.

As an example of the **comm** command, suppose you have two files: **wp**, which lists the names of people in your company who use word processing, and **ss**, which contains the names of people who use spreadsheets. Then **comm -23 wp ss** will tell you who uses word processing, but not spreadsheets; **comm -13 wp ss** will tell you who uses spreadsheets, but not word processing; and **comm -12 wp ss** will tell you who uses both.

If the two files are identical, **comm** returns an exit code of 0 and places all lines in column 3; if the two files have differences, **comm** returns an exit code of 1 and lists lines in all three columns; if one of the files is unreadable, **comm** returns an exit code of 2 and has no output.

Note   Because **comm** compares line by line, it is most suitable for lists or databases stored in files. The command works only on pairs of text files that have been presorted.

See Also   Compare files byte by byte (**cmp**)
Compare files for differences (**diff**)
Sort files (**sort**, Chapter 4)
Discard repeated lines (**uniq**, Chapter 4)

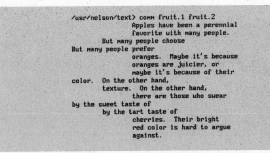

```
/usr/nelson/text> comm fruit.1 fruit.2
                          Apples have been a perennial
                          favorite with many people.
              But many people choose
But many people prefer
                          oranges.  Maybe it's because
                          oranges are juicier, or
                          maybe it's because of their
color.  On the other hand,
              texture.  On the other hand,
                          there are those who swear
by the sweet taste of
              by the tart taste of
                          cherries.  Their bright
                          red color is hard to argue
                          against.
```

Comparing two files with the comm command

Compress Contents of a File

```
$ pack [-] [-f] [file(s)]
$ unpack file(s)
```

Use **pack** to compress the contents of a file, thereby reducing its size by one-quarter to nearly one-half. If compression succeeds, **pack** replaces an original file called *name* with a new compressed file called *name*.**z**. For example, if you enter **pack record**, the result will be a file named **record.z**.

Use **unpack** to decompress a compressed file. It replaces a file called *name*.**z** with another called *name*. For example, if you enter **unpack record.z**, the result will be a file named **record**.

Application   To compress a file called **tables**, enter **pack tables**. The result will be a new file called **tables.z**.

43

You can decompress **tables.z** by entering **unpack tables.z**.

Options   - Toggle display of statistical information
           -f Force compression

Note   The **pack** and **unpack** commands enable you to archive files that you don't expect to modify often.

See Also   Display contents of a compressed file (**pcat**)

Concatenate Files

```
$ cat [-][-su][-v[-et]] [file(s)]
```

This multipurpose command enables you to display the contents of a text file, display several files, concatenate files, copy a file, create a text file, or display invisible control characters.

Application   To display the contents of a text file, enter the command followed by the name of the file, for example, **cat memo**.

To display the contents of several files, enter the command followed by the names of the files, separated by spaces, for example, **cat memo letter** or **cat memo_?**.

If the text scrolls down your screen too fast to read, you can stop it by pressing **Ctrl S**, then resume scrolling by pressing **Ctrl Q**. Another way to avoid this problem is to pipe the output of **cat** to **pg**, which displays text one screen at a time.

To concatenate files (which is the use for which the command is named), enter the command followed by the names of the files to be concatenated, separated by spaces, the redirection to symbol (>), and the name of the target file. Do not use one of the source files as the target file; choose a different file. Otherwise, the file will be wiped out before **cat** has a chance to begin. For example, to concatenate four files called **Q1**, **Q2**, **Q3**, and **Q4**, enter **cat Q1 Q2 Q3 Q4 > 1993**.

To make a copy of a file, enter the command followed by the name of the file to be copied, the redirection to symbol (>), and the name of the new file. For example, to make a copy of **old** called **new**, enter **cat old > new**.

To create a file, enter the command, the redirection to symbol (>), and the name of the file to be created. When you press **Return**, the cursor will drop down to a blank line. Type the text to be placed in the file, then press **Ctrl D** to mark the end of the file. The text you typed will be written to the file, which you can verify by displaying the file with the **cat** command. The following is an example:

```
$ cat > text
This is a text file,
created by the cat
command. Ctrl D
$ cat text
This is a text file,
created by the cat
command.
$ _
```

Suppose you are using a personal computer with a communications program as a terminal on a UNIX system. To download a file to your PC (say, file **info**), turn on the capture feature in your communications program, log into the UNIX system, change to the desired directory, and enter **cat info**.

To upload a file from your PC to the UNIX system and store the contents in a file named **store**, log into the UNIX system, change to the desired directory, enter **cat > store**, turn on the feature that transmits the file on your PC, and press **Ctrl D** after all the text has been sent.

Options

-     Read text from keyboard input. This option enables you to combine text in existing files with keyboard input in any order. The **cat** command interprets the - as another file, which contains the text you type at the keyboard. Press **Ctrl D** to mark the end of the file

-s   Suppress messages about nonexistent files

-u   Unbuffered: characters are displayed one at a time, rather than in blocks (the default)

-v   Display invisible control characters other than newlines, tabs, and formfeeds

-ve   Display invisible control characters other than tabs and formfeeds (newlines appear as dollar signs ($))

45

Copy Files

-vt Display invisible control characters other than
newlines (tabs appear as ^I, formfeeds as ^L)

-vet Display all invisible control characters

Note If you don't provide any filenames, the **cat** command
will read the text you type at your keyboard.

See Also Copy files (**cp**)
Display large files (**more**, **page**, **pg**)
Format files for printing (**pr**, Chapter 6)

```
/usr/nelson/entry> cat market sales > salesmkt
/usr/nelson/entry> ls -l
total 6
-ru-r--r--   1 nelson        283 Apr 27 21:17 market
-ru-r--r--   1 nelson        566 Apr 27 21:25 salesmkt
-ru-r--r--   1 nelson        283 Apr 27 20:41 sales
-ru-r--r--   3 nelson        180 Apr 27 20:38 sample
-ru-r--r--   3 nelson        180 Apr 27 20:38 sample.ln
-ru-r--r--   3 nelson        180 Apr 27 20:38 sample.ln2

/usr/nelson/entry> cat salesmkt > mktsales
/usr/nelson/entry> ls -l
total 7
-ru-r--r--   1 nelson        283 Apr 27 21:17 market
-ru-r--r--   1 nelson        566 Apr 27 21:25 salesmkt
-ru-r--r--   1 nelson        283 Apr 27 20:41 sales
-ru-r--r--   1 nelson        566 Apr 27 21:25 mktsales
-ru-r--r--   3 nelson        180 Apr 27 20:38 sample
-ru-r--r--   3 nelson        180 Apr 27 20:38 sample.ln
-ru-r--r--   3 nelson        180 Apr 27 20:38 sample.ln2
```

Concatenating and copying with the cat command

Copy Files

```
$ cp [-ipr] file_1 file_2
$ cp [-ipr] file(s) dir
$ cp [-ipr] dir_1 dir_2
```

Use **cp** to make a copy of a file, to copy a set of files from one directory
to another, or to make a copy of a directory with all its subdirectories
and files.

Application To make a copy of file **old** called **new**, enter **cp old new**.
If **new** doesn't already exist, **cp** will create it; if it does,
cp will overwrite it. To provide a warning about an
existing file, enter **cp -i old new**. Before proceeding to
make the copy, **cp** will first prompt you for confirmation.

To copy files **memo.past**, **memo.present**, and
memo.future from the current directory to directory
time, enter **cp memo.* time**. If you have write
permission for **time**, the copies will be made.

To make a copy of directory **work** under the same parent, called **backup**, enter **cp -r work backup**. To place the copied directory in **/usr/eng/misc**, enter **cp -r work /usr/eng/misc/backup**. You must have write permission in the target directory.

Options -i Interactive: prompt to confirm before overwriting an existing file

-p Preserve the permissions and time of last modification of the file being copied

-r Recursively copy subdirectories and files

Note You can use the **cp** command to provide simple backup. You can also use it to create a file that is very similar to another, with only a few modifications.

See Also Change file-access permissions (**chmod**)
Change file ownership (**chown**, Chapter 8)
Link a file (**ln**)
Move or rename a file (**mv**)
Delete files (**rm**)

Count Lines, Words, and Characters

```
$ wc [-lwc] [file(s)]
```

Use **wc** to count the number of lines, words, and characters in a text file.

Application To display the number of lines, words, and characters (in that order) in file **test.case** in the current directory, enter **wc test.case**.

To display only the number of words, enter **wc -w test.case**.

Options The three options for **wc** restrict the output to one of the three items:

-l Count only lines (separated by newlines)

-w Count only words (separated by spaces, tabs, and newlines)

-c Count only characters

Note This command is handy for showing you the size of a file in any of three units. If you don't enter a filename, **wc** counts units of your keyboard input.

```
/usr/nelson/entry> wc salesmkt
       8      103      566 salesmkt

/usr/nelson/entry> file salesmkt
salesmkt:        ascii text

/usr/nelson/entry> file sample
sample:          English text
```

Examples of the wc and file commands

Delete Files

```
$ rm [-fir] file(s)
$ rm [-fir] directory(ies) [file(s)]
```

Use **rm** to remove files from a directory or directories from the file system.

Application   To remove files **scratch.1**, **scratch.2**, and **scratch.3** from the current directory, enter **rm scratch.?**. If more than one link already exists for each file, only the link will be removed; if each file has only one link, the text is removed from the disk. You must have write permission in the parent directory.

To remove a directory called **trash**, along with all its subdirectories and files, enter **rm -r trash**. You can also specify the removal of a particular file, or set of files, in a directory. To remove files **bottles**, **cans**, and **plastic** from directory **trash**, enter **rm trash bottles cans plastic**.

To remove all files from directory **refuse** interactively, enter **rm -i refuse ***. Each filename will be displayed, followed by a question mark for confirmation of the deletion. Enter **y** to confirm deletion, **n** (or anything else) to leave the file intact.

Options   -f   Force the removal of files without write permission (dangerous, but may be necessary in some situations)
-i   Interactive: confirm for each file before deleting
-r   Recursively remove subdirectories and files

Notes   Because UNIX has no **unrm** command, be careful with the **rm** command, especially when you're using wildcards. For extra safety, use the interactive option (**-i**). When removing a directory, you have to use the **-r** option.

48

See Also   Change file-access permissions (**chmod**)
Link a file (**ln**)
Delete a directory (**rmdir**, Chapter 2)

Determine Contents of Files

```
$ file [-ch] [-f names] [-m magic] file(s)
```

Use **file** to determine the contents of a file or a set of files.

Application   Suppose you find a file in one of your subdirectories called **mystery**. You don't know whether this file contains source code for a program, ordinary text, or something else. To get an inkling of what it may contain, enter **file mystery**. The command will return a brief description like "ASCII text," "BASIC program text," or "English text."

To check all files in the current directory, enter **file ***. To construct a list of those files that contain some kind of text, enter **file * | grep text**. The **grep** command will reduce the list to those described as containing "text."

Suppose you have a list of filenames stored in a file called **list**. To check the files named, enter **file -f list**. To show only text files, enter **file -f list | grep text**.

The **file** command relies on a cross-reference file called **/etc/magic** for its determinations.

Options   -c   Check your magic file for formatting errors
-f *names*   File *names* contains the names of files to be checked
-h   Do **not** follow symbolic links
-m *magic*   Use *magic* as the magic file instead of **/etc/magic**

Note   The **file** command can give you an educated guess, but is not always correct. It enables you to check a file before attempting to display it on your screen.

See Also   Concatenate a file (**cat**)
Display large files (**pg**)
Link a file (**ln**)
Screen editor (**vi**)

Display Closing Lines

```
$ tail [+[n]bcl] [-f] [-r] file(s)
$ tail [-[n]bcl] [-f] [-r] file(s)
```

Use **tail** to display the closing lines of a file or a set of files, or to monitor processing on a file.

Application   To display the last 10 lines of file **plan**, enter **tail plan** (equivalent to **tail -10 plan**). You will see the last 10 lines (the default).

To display the last 20 lines instead of ten, enter **tail -20 plan**.

To display all lines after line 50, enter **tail +50 plan**.

To follow the growth of file **plan**, enter **tail -f plan**. First, you will see the last 10 lines; then, every second, you will see any new lines appended to **plan**.

Options   -[n]b   Display the last n blocks
+[n]b   Display all blocks after block n
-[n]c   Display the last n characters
+[n]c   Display all characters after character n
-[n]l   Display the last n lines
+[n]l   Display all lines after line n
-f   Follow the growth of the file (either by itself or appended to one of the previous options)
-r   Display the text in reverse order (either by itself or appended to one of the previous options, except -f)

In each instance, the default value for n is 10. Because the default unit for **tail** is lines, l is optional in the options just shown.

Note   If you use **tail** to follow the growth of a file, **tail** will keep following until you stop it. Use **Ctrl D** for a foreground process, **kill** (Chapter 2) for a background process.

See Also   Concatenate files (**cat**)
Display opening lines of a file (**head**)
Display large files (**more, page, pg**)

Display Contents of a Compressed File

```
$ pcat file(s)
```

Use **pcat** to display the contents of a file already compressed by the **pack** command.

Application To display the contents of file **tables.z**, enter **pcat tables.z**.

Note The **pcat** command enables you to view the contents of a compressed file without having to decompress it first.

See Also Compress contents of a file (**pack**)

Display Filename

```
$ basename path[suffix]
```

Use **basename** to read a full pathname and display only the name of the file.

Application To extract the basename from the following pathname, enter **basename /usr/lib/terminfo/a/adm3**. The output will be **adm3**.

Note If the filename includes a suffix, you can also instruct **basename** to truncate the suffix.

Display Large Files

```
$ more [-cdflsuw] [-height] [+line] [+/pattern] file(s)
$ page [-cdflsuw] [-height] [+line] [+/pattern] file(s)
```

Use **more** or **page** to display a large file one screen at a time, using a variety of commands to control the display. The two commands are nearly identical. The **page** command displays one more line of text.

Application To begin displaying a file called **text**, enter **more text**. The first screenful will appear, and you can use a number of commands to change the display.

Options -c   Redraw the display instead of scrolling it
-d   Display instructions with help

51

-f	Do not fold (or truncate) lines that are wider than your screen; count longer lines as one, rather than two lines
-l	Ignore formfeed character (^L), which usually indicates end of page
-s	Compress consecutive blank lines to one blank line
-u	Suppress screen attributes like underlining and high intensity
-w	Prompt before exiting and wait for a key to be pressed
-height	Height of display window in character lines
+line	Start display at line number *line*
+/pattern	Start display two lines short of the first occurrence of the text pattern specified

Once the display appears, press **h** to display the keys available to modify the display. Here are some of the most common options:

f	Go on to the next full screen
p	Previous file
n	Next file
q	Quit: exit **more** or **page**

You can type a number before any of these except **q** to act as a multiplier. For example, press **3f** to move three screenfuls ahead.

Note   When you are displaying a file, the default display at the bottom of the screen is "--More--(*p*%)," where *p* is the percentage of the file already displayed.

See Also   Concatenate files (**cat**)
Display large files (**pg**)

Display Large Files

```
$ pg [-] [-cefnrs] [+line] [+/pattern/] [-n] [-p prompt]
file(s)
```

Use **pg** to display text in a file one screenful at a time, using a number of different commands to move forward or backward in the file.

Application   To display the first page of a file called **text**, enter **pg text**. The first page will appear, and you can use a number of different commands to modify the display.

Options   -c   Clear the screen for each new page of text
-e   Don't prompt and wait at the end of the file
-f   Don't split lines that are too wide for the screen
-n   Process commands without **Return** required
-r   Restricted mode: escape to shell inhibited
-s   Display messages and prompts in reverse video

Press **h** or **?** to display the help screen, which shows the commands available. Here are some of the most common options:

Return	Next page
n **Return**	Go to page *n*
-*n* **Return**	Go back *n* pages
+*n* **Return**	Advance *n* pages
*n*l	Scroll to line *n*
-*n*l	Scroll back *n* lines
+*n*l	Scroll ahead *n* lines
q	Quit: exit from **pg**

Note   This command is more powerful than **cat** but probably a little harder to use than **more** or **page**.

See Also   Concatenate files (**cat**)
Find text in files (**grep**, Chapter 4)
Display opening lines (**head**)
Display closing lines (**tail**)
Display large files (**more**, **page**)

Display Opening Lines

```
$ head [-n] file(s)
```

Use **head** to display the opening lines of any file or set of files.

Application   To display the first 10 lines of file **plan**, enter **head plan**. You will see the first 10 lines (the default).

To display more lines, say 20, enter **head -20 plan**.

Option   -*n*   Display *n* lines instead of the default 10.

Note   You can use this command to take a quick look at the first few lines of a file. The **tail** command lets you look at the last few lines.

See Also   Concatenate files (**cat**)
Display large files (**more**, **page**, **pg**)
Display closing lines (**tail**)

Find Files

```
$ find path(s) criteria action(s)
```

Use **find** to search the directory (or directories) indicated, match filenames to the criteria given, then carry out the action (or actions) specified.

Application   To search the current directory for files that begin with the letters **edc** and display the names on your screen, enter **find . -name 'edc*' -print**. In this example, the path to search is **.** (the current directory), the criterion is **-name 'edc*'**, and the action to be carried out on any files matched is **-print**. (In the world of UNIX, "print" means "display.")

The path you specify can be any directory (or directories) in your file system, including the following:

/   Root (the entire file system)
..   The parent directory
.   The current directory

Next, you can specify any of the following, which restrict the search to files that meet certain criteria:

-name *file*	Find file(s) named *file*
-type *type*	Find file(s) that match the type code:
	f Ordinary file
	d Directory
	b Block device
	c Character device
	p Named pipe (FIFO)
-user *name*	Find file(s) that are owned by *name*
-group *group*	Find file(s) that are owned by *group*
-perm *code*	Find file(s) with permission modes *code*
-newer *file*	Find file(s) that have been modified more recently than *file*

-size *size*	Find file(s) that contain *size*:
	+*k* more than *k* blocks
	k exactly *k* blocks
	-*k* fewer than *k* blocks
-links *links*	Find file(s) that contain *links*:
	+*i* more than *i* links
	i exactly *i* links
	-*i* fewer than *i* links
-ctime *days*	Find file(s) that were changed *days*:
	+*d* more than *d* days ago
	d exactly *d* days ago
	-*d* fewer than *d* days ago
-mtime *days*	Find file(s) that were modified *days*:
	+*d* more than *d* days ago
	d exactly *d* days ago
	-*d* fewer than *d* days ago
-atime *days*	Find file(s) that were accessed *days*:
	+*d* more than *d* days ago
	d exactly *d* days ago
	-*d* fewer than *d* days ago

You can group sets of criteria and apply logical selection by using the following notation:

-a	and
-o	or
\!	not
\(...\)	group together

The action statements you can use with **find** are as follows:

-print	Display the full pathnames of each file matched.
-exec *cmd*	Execute command *cmd* on each file.
-ok *cmd*	Execute command *cmd* on each file—with a prompt to confirm.
-depth	Copy each directory along with its files (used only with, and before, **-cpio**).
-cpio *path*	Copy to the device indicated by *path* each file matched, using **cpio** format.

To locate all **core** files in your file system, enter the command line **find / -name core -print**. To get rid of all

Link a File

those **core** files that haven't been accessed in more than a week (with a prompt to confirm), enter **find / -name core -atime +7 -ok rm {} \;**.

To copy to tape all files in directory **/usr** that contain source code for either C programs or FORTRAN programs that haven't been modified in the past 30 days, enter the command line, **find /usr \(-name '*.c' -o -name '*.f' \) -mtime +30 | cpio -oc > /dev/rmt/mt2**.

Note The **find** command enables you to display a set of files that meet certain criteria, examine the list, then copy, move, or delete those files. It can traverse an entire file system in its relentless search for files.

See Also Change file-access permissions (**chmod**)
Copy in and out (**cpio**)

Link a File

```
$ ln [-fns] file_1 file_2
$ ln [-fns] files directory
```

In a UNIX system, a file may be known by more than one name. Each name is called a *link* to the file. No matter how many links exist, there is still just one file. The **ln** command enables you to create links in one of two ways:

- You can create one link to a single file, using either a different name or the same name in a different directory

- You can create a set of links to a set of files, using all the same names in a different directory

Application To create a link named **newname** to a file currently named **original**, enter the following command line:

```
ln original newname
```

To create a link to each of a set of files called **memo.01**, **memo.02**, **memo.03**, **memo.04**, and **memo.05** and place the links in directory **/usr/mktg/prod/news**, enter the following command:

```
ln memo.* /usr/mktg/prod/news
```

The **ln** command will create five links called **memo.01**, **memo.02**, **memo.03**, **memo.04**, and **memo.05** in directory **/usr/mktg/prod/news**.

Options

-f Force creation of the link even if it means overwriting an existing file or overriding access permissions

-n Do not overwrite an existing file

-s Create a symbolic link

Notes

If you don't use any arguments, or if you use either **-f** or **-n**, you create a *hard link*. If you use the **-s** option, you create a *soft link (symbolic link)*.

You can create a hard link to an ordinary file but not to a directory. You can create a hard link in a different directory but not in a different file system. You can create a symbolic link either to a directory or in a different file system.

If you have to remove a link, you can use the **rm** command.

See Also

Copy files (**cp**)
Move or rename a file (**mv**)
Delete files (**rm**)
Display filenames in a directory (**ls**)
Change file-access permissions (**chmod**)
Change file ownership (**chown**, Chapter 8)

Move or Rename a File

```
$ mv [-if] file(s) directory
$ mv [-if] file_1 file_2
$ mv [-if] directory_1 directory_2
```

Use **mv** to move a file or a set of files to a different directory, or to rename a file or directory.

Application To move a single file or a set of files from your working directory to another directory, use the first form of the command line. For example, to move **work.a**, **work.b**, and **work.c** from the current directory to directory **plans** in the same parent directory, enter **mv work.? ../plans**.

To rename a file, use the second form of the command line. For example, to change the name of a file in your working directory currently called **bigcat** to **tiger**, enter **mv bigcat tiger**. Renaming a directory is nearly the same.

Options   -f Force the move
              -i Interactive: confirm before overwriting the target file

Note   Before executing, the **mv** command checks the target file to make sure you have write permission.

See Also Copy files (**cp**)
              Link a file (**ln**)
              Change file-access permissions (**chmod**)

Split a File

```
$ split [-][-n] [file] [name]
```

Use **split** to split a file called *file* into smaller files, based solely on line count. You can specify the number of lines to be allocated to each smaller file; you can also specify the base name of each smaller file.

Application Suppose you have a file called **large** that is 3,627 lines long. If you enter **split large**, the output will be four files called **xaa**, **xab**, **xac**, and **xad**. The first three files will contain 1,000 lines each; the fourth will contain 627 lines.

The default number of lines is 1,000; the default names are **xaa**, **xab**, **xac**, and so on. But you are free to use other values. To split **large** into 500-line files with names that begin with **small**, you can enter **split -500 large small**. This time, the output will be eight files called **smallaa**, **smallab**, **smallac**, ..., and **smallah**. Each of the first seven files will contain 500 lines; the eighth will contain 127.

To split up a segment of text that you enter at the keyboard, you can enter **split -** and begin typing. This doesn't seem like a very useful feature, but you can use it.

Note   Some commands will not accept large files. You can use **split** to provide these commands with acceptable files for processing.

See Also Split files by context (**csplit**)

Split a File by Context

```
$ csplit [-][-fprefix] [-ks] file argument(s)
```

Use **csplit** to split a file into smaller files either by size or by context. You can instruct **csplit** either to count lines or to look for expressions.

Application Suppose you have a large file called **novel** that is hundreds of pages long. Suppose the file contains 36 chapters, each beginning with the expression "Chapter 1," "Chapter 2," and so on, to "Chapter 36." To split this file into chapters, you can enter **csplit novel '/^Chapter /' {37}**.

The output will be 37 files called **xx00, xx01, xx02, ..., xx36**. The first file, **xx00**, contains all text that precedes the first chapter (such as a Foreword or Preface). Each of the remaining files contains exactly one chapter.

The command line instructs **csplit** to look for the word "Chapter," followed by a space, at the beginning of a line (^), 36 times. If you don't know the exact number of chapters, you can play it safe by using a larger number (such as 40) and including the **-k** option. Then the command line will look like this: **csplit -k novel '/^Chapter /' {40}**.

If you want to use a prefix other than **xx**, you can specify another with the **-f** option. Then the command line will look like this: **csplit -k -fromance novel '/^Chapter /' {40}**. The output will be smaller files named **romance00, romance01, romance02, ..., romance36**.

Options -fprefix   Use *prefix* instead of **xx** prefix for filenames
  -k   Do not remove the files created if all conditions are not met
  -s   Suppress character counts for smaller files

The following may be used to specify the locations of splits:

  /*expr*/   Create a file that begins at the current line and ends one line short of the next occurrence of expression *expr*. You can end the file *l* lines shorter by appending -*l* or *l* lines further by appending +*l*.

%expr%	Same as */expr/* except that no file is created.
line	Create a file that begins at the current line and ends one line short of line number *line*.
{n}	Repeat factor: repeat the previous argument *n* times. For example, **500 {20}** means to split the source file into twenty 500-line subfiles.

Note   The **csplit** command offers more flexibility than **split** but is also much more complex to use.

See Also   Split a file (**split**)

4

Text and Number Processing

This chapter describes commands you can use to perform calculations or to locate, sort, rearrange, manipulate, or move text in files. Some of these commands are simple to learn and execute. Others include a wide variety of features to choose from and require more time to learn.

Change Format

$ newform [-a*n*] [-b*n*] [-c*x*] [-e*n*] [-f] [-i *fmt*] [-l*n*] [-o *fmt*] [-p*n*] [-s] [*file(s)*]

Use **newform** to change the format of text files in various ways. You can add characters, remove characters, change tab settings, and so on.

Application To remove 12 characters from the end of each line of file **wide**, enter **newform -e12 wide**

Options
-a*n*	Append *n* characters to the end of each line
-b*n*	Remove *n* characters from the beginning of each line
-c*x*	Set the prefix or suffix character to *x* (space by default)
-e*n*	Remove *n* characters from the end of each line
-f	Write the tab format before the output (**-8** by default)
-i*fmt*	Set the tab format (**-8** by default)
-l*n*	Set line length to *n* character positions (**72** by default)
-o*fmt*	Convert tabs to spaces (**-8** by default)
-p*n*	Prefix *n* characters to the beginning of each line
-s	Remove characters before the first tab; append as many as 8 to the end of the line

Note This command enables you to make quick, easy formatting changes.

See Also Edit stream of text (**sed**)

Concatenate Files Horizontally

```
$ paste [-] [-s] [-d[list]] file(s)
```

Use **paste** to paste files next to each other side by side. You can also use the command to obtain a multicolumn display or serial output (with all newlines removed).

Application   To paste name to address in two columns, with items on each line separated by tabs, enter **paste name address**.

To display the names of the files in the current directory in five columns, enter **ls | paste - - - - -**.

To remove all newlines and produce a single line of output, separated by slashes, enter **paste -s -d'\/' name address**.

Options   -   Read a line from the standard input (either the keyboard or input from a pipe)

-d_list_   Field separator (or delimiter). If you omit this option entirely, a tab is used; if you omit _list_, no delimiter at all is used (the columns are pushed together). You can make a list, which **paste** will rotate if there are more columns than delimiters. Here are a few possibilities:

'\t'	tab
'\\'	backslash
'\ |'	vertical bar
'\n'	newline
-s	Serial output: one line without newlines

Note   The most common use of **paste** is to perform horizontal concatenation. But you can also arrange input into columns or arrange columns into a single serial stream.

See Also   Cut fields from a file (**cut**)
Find text in files (**grep**)
Prepare a file for printing (**pr**, Chapter 6)

```
/usr/nelson/new> cat > name
Adams
Bates
Cairn
Dempsey
Edison

/usr/nelson/new> cat > phone
(415) 328-7714
(408) 247-0089
(415) 325-8823
(408) 268-8734
(213) 243-6745


/usr/nelson/new> paste name phone
Adams    (415) 328-7714
Bates    (408) 247-0089
Cairn    (415) 325-8823
Dempsey  (408) 268-8734
Edison   (213) 243-6745
```

An example of the paste command

Cut Fields from a File

```
$ cut -clist [list(s)]
$ cut -flist [-dc] [-s] [list(s)]
```

Use **cut** to display selected columns or fields from a file. *Columns* are single character positions on a line; *fields* are sets of characters separated by tabs.

Application   To display columns 1, 2, 3, 5, and 9 of file **info**, enter **cut -c1-3,5,9 info**. To display fields 1, 4, 5, and 6 of file **info**, enter **cut -f1,4-6 info**.

To display fields 5, 6, and 7 of the **/etc/passwd** file (full name, home directory, and login shell), enter **cut -f5-7 -d: /etc/passwd**. Because the fields of this file are separated by colons (:) instead of tabs, the **-d** option is required.

Options   -c*list*   Select for display the columns indicated by *list*

           -f*list*   Select for display the fields indicated by *list*

           -d*c*   Replace tab with *c* as the field separator (or delimiter)

           -s   Suppress lines with field separators

           list   Nonconsecutive numbers separated by commas or consecutive numbers indicated by hyphens (or a combination of both)

Note You can use this command to select information from a file and use it to construct a new file.

See Also Find text in files (**grep**)
Join two relations (**join**)
Concatenate files horizontally (**paste**)
Prepare files for printing (**pr**)

Desk Calculator

```
$ dc [file]
```

Use **dc** to perform arithmetic calculations.

Application Enter **dc** to start the calculator. Then you can use the following functions, keeping in mind that you enter both numbers before performing a calculation:

n	Enter *n*
+	Add last number to previous number
-	Subtract last number from previous number
*	Multiply last number by previous number
/	Divide last number into previous number
p	Display ("print") the most recent result
q	Quit; exit from the calculator

You can also combine operators, as in the following examples:

5+p	Add 5 to the previous number and display the result
3-p	Subtract 3 from the previous number and display the result

Note The **dc** command performs the more basic functions, along with changing number bases, scaling, functions, subscripts, and logical control. However, for a wider variety of functions and easier use, refer to the **bc** command.

See Also High-precision calculator (**bc**)

```
/usr/nelson/new> dc
7
5+p
12
3-p
9
q
```

A short session with the dc command

Discard Repeated Lines

`$ uniq [-cdu] [-n] [+m] [input [output]]`

Use **uniq** to report repeated lines and discard extra duplicate lines.

Application   Suppose you have a file called **list**, with the following contents:

```
ape
ape
ape
banana
banana
```

To eliminate the extra duplicate lines, enter **uniq list**. The result will be as follows:

```
$ uniq list
ape
banana
$ _
```

Options   -c   Count; precede each line with the number of times it occurs in the file

-d   Delete all but the first in a sequence of duplicate lines

-u   Unique; display only lines that occur once

-n Skip the first n fields in a line

+m Skip the first m characters in a field

Field separators are spaces and tabs.

Note   No input or output file is required for **uniq**. It is most often used in a pipe with other commands, using sorted input.

See Also   Sort lines in a file (**sort**)

```
/usr/nelson/new> cat > fruits
apple
apple
apple
banana
banana
banana
banana
cherry
cherry
cherry
cherry
cherry
date
date
date
date
date
date
/usr/nelson/new> uniq fruits
apple
banana
cherry
date
```

An example of the uniq command

Edit Stream of Text

```
$ sed [-e script] [-f file] [-n] [file(s)]
```

Use **sed** to perform editing on large files noninteractively. The **sed** command takes its input from a file or from the standard input, searches for text, makes changes, and writes the result to the standard output.

A set of **sed** commands is called a *script*. You can provide a script either on the command line or in a separate file. Each command in the script specifies lines in the input file to be modified (called *addresses*), then the functions to be performed on those lines.

Application   To change every occurrence of "DOS" to "UNIX" in a file called **system**, enter the following command line, with the script enclosed in single quotes:

```
$ sed -e 's/DOS/UNIX/g' system
```

A second way to accomplish the same thing is to place the script in a file, then invoke the filename on the command line, as shown here:

```
$ cat script
s/DOS/UNIX/g
$ sed -f script system
. . .
$
```

If no address is given, as in the example previously shown, **sed** processes every line of the input file. If an address is given, it precedes the command and restricts processing to the lines indicated. Each address, or range of addresses, is of the form [*addr_1*[,*addr_2*]]. Each individual address can be one of the following:

n	A line number
/*expr*/	An expression to be matched on a line
.	The current line
$	The last line in the file

An expression *expr* used to specify an address can contain \n to indicate a newline.

The **sed** command reads each line of the input file into a temporary buffer called the *pattern space*. It applies any commands that apply to the text in the pattern space. To allow additional processing on the text, you can copy the text in the pattern space to a second buffer called the *hold space*.

The commands you can use are listed here. Each is preceded by a number that indicates the maximum number of addresses allowed.

[1]a\	
text	Append *text* on the following line
[2]b*label*	Branch to :*label*
[2]c\	
text	Change to *text*
[2]d	Delete everything in the pattern space
[2]D	Delete only the first line of the pattern space
[2]g	Replace everything in the pattern space with the contents of the hold space
[2]G	Append text in the hold space to the text in the pattern space
[2]h	Replace everything in the hold space with the contents of the pattern space

[2]H	Append text in the pattern space to the text in the hold space
[1]i\	
text	Insert *text* on the previous line
[2]l	Write (list) the contents of the pattern space to the standard output
[2]n	Copy the contents of the pattern space to the standard output
[2]N	Append the input line to the pattern space, separated by a newline
[2]p	Display (print) the contents of the pattern space on the standard output
[2]P	Display (print) the first line of the pattern space on the standard output
[1]q	Quit: branch to the end of the **sed** script
[2]r *file*	Copy the contents of *file* to the standard output

[2]s/*expr_1*/*expr_2*/*flags* Substitute *expr_2* for *expr_1* as indicated by *flags*:

g	Global: all occurrences
n	*n*th occurrence only
p	Display (print) the contents of the pattern space if a replacement was made
w *file*	Write the contents of the pattern space to *file* if a replacement was made

[2]t *label*	Branch to :*label* if substitutions have been made
[2]w *file*	Write the contents of the pattern space to *file*
[2]x	Exchange contents of the pattern and hold spaces
[2]y/*str_1*/*str_2*/	Replace each character in *str_1* with the corresponding character in *str_2* (two strings of equal length)
[2]!*command*	Apply *command* to any line not matched
[0]:*label*	Each *label* provides a branching point for **b** and **t** commands (1-8 characters)
[1]=	Write the input line to the standard output
[2]{	
script	
}	Execute the commands in the script on each line matched

Options	-e *script*	Execute the script entered on the command line
	-f *file*	Execute the script stored in *file*
	-n	Do not write each line of the input file to the standard output

Note Except for its usefulness in fairly simple substitutions, the **sed** command is horrendously complicated and confusing. If at all possible, use another command instead.

See Also Find text in a file (**grep**)

Encrypt Text

```
$ crypt [keyword] [-k]
```

Use **crypt** to encrypt text in a file and store it in another file. You can also read from the encrypted file with **crypt**.

Application To encrypt the text in a file called **memo** and store the result in a file called **MEMO**, enter **crypt < memo > MEMO**. You will be prompted for the keyword. Once you've entered the keyword and encrypted the text, the next step is to delete the original file (**memo**).

To view the cleartext, enter **crypt < MEMO** and enter the keyword again.

Options The **crypt** command has two options, but it isn't advisable to use either one of them:

-k	Use the keyword assigned to environmental variable CRYPTKEY
keyword	Enter *keyword* directly on your command line.

Notes The best way to use **crypt** is to have the command prompt you for the keyword. If you assign the keyword to CRYPTKEY or enter it on a command line, you run the risk of revealing it to system intruders.

All UNIX text editors have options for reading encrypted files.

See Also Screen editor (**vi**)

Find Text in Files

```
$ grep [-bchilnsv] pattern file(s)
$ fgrep [-bchilnsvx] [-e string] [-f file] pattern file(s)
$ egrep [-bchilnsv] [-e expr] [-f file] pattern file(s)
```

Use **grep** to search for text in files, or in the standard input, then display each line matched on the standard output. If **grep** searches more than one file, it precedes each line by the name of the file in which it was found.

A fast version called **fgrep** and an extended version called **egrep** are similar to the original command, **grep**. The two derived versions differ in a few options and in the kind of text they can search for. Each program can match the following:

fgrep   Literal strings only
grep   Strings and regular expressions
egrep   Compound expressions

Application   To search for lines in a file called **table** that contain the word "text," enter **grep text table**. Just to count the number of lines in which a match is found, enter **grep -c text table**.

If the text you are searching for contains spaces, you have to enclose it in double quotes. To search the same file for "new text," enter the following: **grep "new text" table**.

Suppose the expression **new text** occurs in several different files, called **memo, report**, and **study**. To search for the expression in all three files, enter **grep "new text" memo report study**. To display only the names of the files that contain the expression, enter **grep -l "new text" memo report study**.

Options   **-b**   Precede each line with its block number
-c   Count; display only the number of lines matched
-h   Suppress filenames
-i   Ignore case
-l   Display only filenames, not lines of text
-n   Precede each line matched with its line number
-s   Suppress file error messages
-v   Invert; match lines in which the text is not found

*Used by **fgrep** only:*

-**e** *string*   Match text that begins with a hyphen
-**f** *file*   Read strings from *file*
-**x**   Match only entire lines

*Used by **egrep** only:*

-**e** *expr*   Match text that begins with a hyphen
-**f** *file*   Read expressions from *file*

Note   You can use **grep** to locate lines in a file where text is found, then pipe the result to another command.

See Also Edit stream of text (**sed**)

```
/usr/nelson/entry> grep color fruit.1
color.  On the other hand,
red color is hard to argue
/usr/nelson/entry> _
```

An example of the grep command

High-Precision Calculator

```
$ bc [-cl] [file(s)]
```

Use **bc** when you want to obtain precise results; convert numbers from one base to another; allow up to 99 places after the decimal point; or take advantage of variables, arrays, functions, and comments.

Application Enter **bc** to begin a session with the calculator. If you have functions stored in files, you can enter the filenames on the command line.

Once you've entered the command, you can use many expressions, including the following:

$a + b$ Add a to b and display the result
$a - b$ Subtract b from a and display the result
$a * b$ Multiply a by b and display the result
a / b Divide b into a and display the result

sqrt(*c*)	Take the square root of *c* and display the result
scale = *s*	Display *s* places after the decimal point
define *z*(*n*) {	Define function *z* with argument *n*
auto *i*	Make variable *i* automatic
...	Function definition
return(*i*)	Function *z* returns a value of *i*
}	End of function
quit	Quit: exit from the calculator

Here is a sample session with **bc**:

```
$ bc
12 + 19
31
37 - 19
18
9 * 6
54
84 / 7
12
sqrt(64)
8
quit
$ _
```

If you want to use any of the special functions, begin the session with **bc -l** instead of **bc**.

Options   -c Compile only—used with at least one filename
           -l Invoke the math library, which includes the following functions:

s	sine
c	cosine
a	arctangent
e	exponential, base e
l	natural logarithm
j(n,x)	Bessel function

Note   You can also convert numbers from one base to another and increase the number of places after the decimal point.

See Also   Disk calculator (**dc**)

```
/usr/nelson/entry> bc
12 + 19
31
37 - 19
18
9 * 6
54
84 / 7
12
sqrt (64)
8
sqrt (75)
8
quit
```

A short session with the bc command

Join Two Relations

```
$ join [-an][-e str][-jn m][-o list][-tc] file_1 file_2
```

Use **join** to perform a relational join function on two presorted files, using a key field that is common to each file. Each file must have been sorted on its key field before you can use the **join** command. Each time the two key fields match, **join** merges the corresponding lines.

Application   Suppose you have two files called **name** and **phone**:

```
$ cat name        $ cat phone
1 John            1 555-1234
2 Mary            2 555-2345
3 Tina            3 555-3456
```

To join the two files, enter **join name phone**. The result will be as follows:

```
$ join name phone
1 John 555-1234
2 Mary 555-2345
3 Tina 555-3456
```

In the example, the line number is common to each file. Therefore, **join** uses the line number as the key field.

Options   -a*n*   Generate in a file named *n* a line for each line in *file_n* not matched in the other file (*n* must be either 1 or 2)

-e *str*   Replace empty fields in the output with *str*

-j*n* *m*   Join on the *m*th field of *file_n*

-o *list*   Specify output fields; each item in *list*, separated by spaces, must be of the form *n.m* (file.field)

-t*c*   Use character *c* as a field separator instead of the default (spaces, tabs, newlines)

Note   You usually use the **join** command to join two files that contain information in tabular form.

See Also   Text-processing language (**awk**, Chapter 8)
Compare files line by line (**comm**, Chapter 3)
Cut fields from a file (**cut**)
Concatenate files horizontally (**paste**)
Sort files (**sort**)
Discard duplicate lines (**uniq**)

Set Line-Numbering

```
$ nl [-btype] [-dxy] [-ftype] [-htype] [-in] [-ln] [-nfmt]
[-p] [-sc] [-vn] [-wn] [file]
```

Use **nl** to insert line numbers in front of lines of text, using either a file or the standard input. By default, **nl** regards all lines as body text on each page.

Application   To number the lines of file **test**, enter **nl test**.

If your file contains a header, body, and footer on each page, you can inform **nl** of this by embedding the following symbols in the file:

\:\:\:   Start of header
\:\:   Start of body
\:   Start of footer

To number all text lines, headers, and footers in file **test**, enter **nl -ba -ht -ft test**.

Options   -b*type*   Body: number lines as indicated by *type*:

a   All lines
n   No lines
p*str*   Only lines that contain string *str*
t   Only lines that contain text (default)

-d*xy*   Change the delimiter for logical page sections (\: by default)

-f*type*   Footer: like **-b**, except the default is n

-h*type*	Header: like **-b**, except the default is n
-i*n*	Increment page numbering by *n* (1 by default)
-l*n*	Compress *n* blank lines to one (1 by default); used with **-ha**, **-ba**, **-fa**, as required
-n*fmt*	Set line numbers according to *fmt*:

	ln	Left-justified, no zeros
	rn	Right-justified, no zeros (default)
	rz	Right-justified, zero-filled

-p	Do not start numbering each new page at 1
-s*c*	Separate line numbers from text with *c* (tab by default)
-v*n*	Start numbering at *n* (1 by default)
-w*n*	Width of number field is *n* (6 by default)

Note   The **nl** command is probably most useful for legal documents and source code for programs.

See Also   Prepare text for printing (**pr**)

```
/usr/nelson/entry> nl fruit.1
     1  Apples have been a perennial
     2  favorite with many people.
     3  But many people prefer
     4  oranges.  Maybe it's because
     5  oranges are juicier, or
     6  maybe it's because of their
     7  color.  On the other hand,
     8  there are those who swear
     9  by the sweet taste of
    10  cherries.  Their bright
    11  red color is hard to argue
    12  against.
```

An example of the nl command

Sort Lines in a File

```
$ sort [-] [-bcdfimMnru] [-ofile] [-tx] [-yk] [-zr]
[+col [-col]] [file(s)]
```

Use **sort** to sort lines in a file or a set of files (or the standard input). You can sort text or numbers with a wide variety of options. If you name more than one file, **sort** merges the files before sorting.

Application To sort the lines in file **study** and display the result on the screen, enter **sort study**.

Sort Lines in a File

To select a specific field, or set of fields, in the file, the **sort** command has its own notation:

+*f* Begin sorting after field *f*
-*g* Stop sorting after field *g*

For example, **+2 -3** on a **sort** command line means to sort only field 3, whereas **+1 -4** means to sort fields 2, 3, and 4.

You can also begin or end a sort in the middle of a field by adding a decimal point and another number to represent character positions in the field. For example, **+3.10 -5.16** means to begin sorting at the eleventh character of field 3 and stop after the sixteenth character of field 5. Default field separators are spaces and tabs.

Options

-**b**   Ignore leading spaces and tabs
-**c**   Make sure the input file has already been sorted
-**d**   Sort in dictionary order (compare only blanks, digits, and letters of the alphabet)
-**f**   Fold uppercase into lowercase (making SORT, Sort, and sort identical during a sort)
-**i**   Ignore invisible characters in sorting
-**m**   Merge only (the files have already been sorted)
-**M**   Months; sort the names of the months in the correct order, not in alphabetical order (-**b** used automatically)
-**n**   Numeric; sort a field as numeric, allowing for minus signs, zeros, and decimal points (-**b** used automatically)
-**o***file* Redirect the output to *file* instead of the standard output (equivalent to > *file*)
-**r**   Sort in reverse order
-**t***x*   Use *x* (any character) as the field separator
-**u**   Unique output: if two or more identical lines result, use only the first
-**y***k*   Set aside *k* kilobytes of memory for the sort
-**z***n*   Allow a maximum of *n* characters per line of input
+*f* [-*g*] Sort only fields *f*+1 through *g*

Note

You can sort either a file, a set of files, or the standard input with the **sort** command. The result can be in alphabetical or numeric order (or reverse order).

Join two relations (**join**)
Discard duplicate lines (**uniq**)

```
/usr/nelson/new> cat list
Adams    (415) 328-7714
Bates    (408) 247-0089
Cairn    (415) 325-8823
Dempsey  (408) 268-8734
Edison   (213) 243-6745

/usr/nelson/new> sort +1 list
Edison   (213) 243-6745
Bates    (408) 247-0089
Dempsey  (408) 268-8734
Cairn    (415) 325-8823
Adams    (415) 328-7714
```

Sorting by telephone number using sort

Translate Characters

```
$ tr [-cds] [str_1] [str_2]
```

Use **tr** to translate characters as indicated by a pair of strings. Options
enable you to select characters *not* named, delete characters, or compress repetitions of a character to a single instance.

Because the syntax for **tr** does not provide for filenames, you have to use
redirection to name input and output files. Otherwise, **tr** uses standard
input and output.

Application To change the numbering of the steps in file steps from 1,
2, 3 to a, b, c, enter **tr 123 abc < steps** (or **tr 1-3 a-c <
steps**). The new numbering will appear on the screen.

To change all letters in **steps** to uppercase and store the
result in **STEPS**, enter **tr "[a-z]" "[A-Z]" < steps >
STEPS**.

To compress multiple occurrences of any character in
repeat to one occurrence, enter **tr -s < repeat**. (This will
translate "HHHHHeeeelp!!!!!" into "Help!".)

To delete all beeps from a file called **annoying** and store
the result in a file called **pleasant**, enter **tr -d "[\007]" <
annoying > pleasant**. (In the world of small computers,
007 is the ASCII code for BEL, the control character that
makes your terminal beep. Sorry, James Bond.)

Options

-c   Use the complement of the characters indicated by *str_1* (that is, use all characters not indicated)

-d   Delete all characters indicated by *str_1*

-s   Squeeze: compress repetitions of a character to one

String notation:

[*x-y*]   A range of characters from *x* to *y*

[*c*n*]   Character *c* repeated *n* times; if *n* is omitted or is zero, it matches the entire corresponding string

asc   ASCII code *asc* (required for characters that cannot be typed from a keyboard)

Note   Although **tr** is capable of many unusual and surprising results, it's usually used for ordinary tasks like converting to uppercase.

See Also   Edit stream of text (**sed**)

5

Text Editing and Formatting

In word-processing software, text editing and formatting are combined in a single program. In the UNIX system, text editing and formatting are two separate functions. You use one program to edit text and another to format it. This chapter covers both types of programs.

The formatting programs include the general-purpose formatters **nroff**, **troff**, and the **mm** macro package, as well as specialized programs like the column filter **col**, the equation and table preprocessors **eqn** and **tbl**, and the PostScript postprocessor **dpost**.

Column Filter

```
$ col [-bfpx]
```

Ordinarily, a printer must reverse motion (that is, perform reverse linefeeds) to print multiple columns. For the benefit of printers that cannot reverse motion (and for video monitors), use **col** in a pipeline between **nroff** and the standard output (**lp** or your screen) to rearrange the text for multiple columns. You also have to use **col** whenever you create boxed text with the **tbl** preprocessor.

Application   One way to pass a text file to **col** for processing is to pipe it from **cat** or **pr**. For example, to display the text on your screen, enter **cat sample | col**. To print the text, enter **cat sample | col | lp**.

Another way to do the same thing is to use redirection. To display the text on your screen, enter **col < sample**. To print the text, enter **col < sample | lp**.

If you are using the **mm** macro package, you won't see the **col** command; you just use the **-c** option on the command line. Here is an example of column filtering to an ordinary line printer:

```
$ mm -c -Tlp part.5 | lp
```

Column Filter

If you are using **nroff**, insert **col** in the pipeline between the command and the destination. Here is an example of column filtering to a DASI 300:

```
$ nroff -T300 part.5 | col | lp
```

Options

- **-b**   The printer cannot backspace
- **-f**   Half-linefeed is permitted
- **-p**   Accept unknown escape sequences
- **-x**   Do not convert spaces to tabs

Character conversion:

The **col** command converts the following eight control characters and three escape sequences:

Name		Character(s)	ASCII Code (Octal)	
BS	Backspace	Ctrl H	010	
HT	Tab	Ctrl I	011	
LF	Linefeed	Ctrl J	012	
VT	Vertical Tab	Ctrl K	013	
CR	Carriage Return	Ctrl M	015	
SO	Start of Text	Ctrl N	016	
SI	End of Text	Ctrl O	017	
SP	Space		040	
	Reverse linefeed	Esc 7	033	067
	Reverse half-linefeed	Esc 8	033	070
	Forward half-linefeed	Esc 9	033	071

Notes

The **col** command can read only from the standard input and write only to the standard output. Therefore, it can process only those files passed to it by way of redirection or a pipe.

The **col** command usually works best when you specify the name of the printer.

See Also

Format tables (**tbl**)
Format text (**mm**)
Format text (**nroff**)

Format Equations

```
$ eqn file | troff [| col] | lp
$ neqn file | nroff [| col] | lp
$ mm -e file [| col] | lp
```

Use **eqn** to format equations for **troff** or **neqn** to format equations for **nroff**.

Application Begin by inserting the appropriate formatting requests into the file. Then execute **eqn** (or **neqn**) to process the file and pipe the output to **troff** (or **nroff**). For example, suppose your source file, called **algebra**, contains the following text:

```
.P
```

Begin with this equation:

```
.EQ I
y ^ = ^ x sup 2 + x - 6
.EN
.P
```

Factor the right side:

```
.EQ I
y ^ = ^ (x + 3)(x - 2)
.EN
```

You can format this text on your screen with **nroff** by using one of the following command lines:

```
$ neqn algebra | nroff -cm | col | more
```

or

```
$ mm -e algebra | col | more
```

You can format this text with **troff** and print it by using the following command line:

```
$ eqn algebra | troff -cm | col | lp
```

Options *Formatting requests:*

.EQ	Begin equation centered (the default)
.EQ I	Begin equation indented
.EQ L	Begin equation flush left
over	Place the preceding expression over the following expression to form a fraction

sup	The expression that follows is an exponent
sub	The expression that follows is a subscript
sqrt	The expression that follows is to appear under a radical
~	Leave a blank space
^	Leave a blank half-space

Note

With **neqn** and **nroff**, the symbols are approximated. With **eqn** and **troff**, the resulting equations are printed with great precision. In addition, **eqn** and **troff** can handle limits, summation and integral signs, vectors, matrices, and tall brackets.

With **mm**, you never actually see the **neqn** command, just the **-e** option on the command line.

See Also

Format text (**mm**)
Format text (**nroff, troff**)

```
/usr/nelson/test> cat > algebra
.P
Begin with this equation:
.EQ I
y ^ = ^ x sup 2 + x - 6
.EN
.P
Factor the right side:
.EQ I
y ^ = ^ (x + 3)(x - 2)
.EN

/usr/nelson/test> neqn algebra | nroff -cm
Begin with this equation:
    y=x2+x-6

Factor the right side:
    y=(x+3)(x-2)
```

An example of the neqn command

Format Tables

```
$ tbl file | troff [| col] | lp
$ mm -t file [| col] | lp
```

Use **tbl** to format text in tables of many columns.

Application Begin by inserting the appropriate formatting requests into the file. The requests include table start, positioning of the table on the page, positioning of the column headings, positioning of the column information, the actual headings, the actual column information, and table end.

With the request in place, use **tbl** to process the file and pipe the output to **troff** (or **nroff**). For example, suppose your source file, called **info**, contains the following text:

```
.P
The information is summarized in the following table.
.TS
center ;
c c c
l l n .
Name Sequence Codes
.sp 1
Reverse line feed       Esc 7   033 067
Reverse half line feed  Esc 8   033 070
Forward half line feed  Esc 9   033 071
.TE
```

You can format this text on your screen with **tbl** and **nroff** using one of the following command lines:

```
$ tbl info | nroff -cm | more
```

or

```
$ mm -t info | more
```

You can format the text with **troff** and print it using the following command line:

```
$ tbl info | troff -cm | lp
```

Options

Formatting requests:

.TS	Table start
center	Center the table
box	Box the table
allbox	Box the table and each individual entry
;	End of the overall layout for the table
l l l	Left-justify each of three headings
c c c	Center each of three headings
r r r	Right-justify each of three headings
l l l	Left-justify each column of information
n n n	Enter each column of information as numeric
r r r	Right-justify each column of information

End of information about the headings; start of the actual entries

Actual column headings, separated by tabs

.sp 1   Optional space between headings and information

Actual information, separated by tabs

.TE   Table end

Notes   When you use **tbl** and **troff**, the resulting tables are printed with great precision. With **tbl** and **nroff**, the tables are approximate.

With **mm**, you never actually see the **tbl** command, just the **-t** option on the command line.

See Also   Format text (**mm**)

Format text (**nroff, troff**)

```
/usr/nelson/test> cat > info
.P
The information is summarized in the following table.
.TS
center ;
c c c
l l n .
Name      Sequence        Codes
.sp 1
Reverse line feed         Esc 7    033 067
Reverse half line feed    Esc 8    033 070
Forward half line feed    Esc 9    033 071
.TE

/usr/nelson/test> tbl info | nroff -cm
The information is summarized in the following table.
                          Name      Sequence   Codes

              Reverse line feed       Esc 7    033 067
              Reverse half line feed  Esc 8    033 070
              Forward half line feed  Esc 9    033 071
```

An example of the tbl command

Format Text

```
$ mm [-cdEty] [-12] [-Tname] file(s)
```

Use **mm** to format text for printing. It enables you to produce paragraphs, lists, displays, headings, headers, footers, footnotes, and so on. The formatting commands must be embedded in the file before you enter the **mm** command to carry out formatting.

Application   To display formatting for file **letter** on the screen, enter **mm letter**. If the file is long, you can enter **mm letter | page** or **mm letter | more**. To format and print **letter**, enter **mm letter | lp** (or **mm letter | pr | lp**).

To print text that contains tables but no equations, enter one of the following command lines:

```
$ mm -t -T37 info | lp (col not required)
$ mm -t -c -T40 info | lp (col required)
```

To print text that contains equations but no tables, enter one of the following command lines:

```
$ mm -e -T37 info | lp (col not required)
$ mm -e -c -T40 info | lp (col required)
```

To print text that contains tables and equations, enter one of the following command lines:

```
$ mm -t -e -T37 info | lp (col not required)
$ mm -t -e -c -T40 info | lp (col required)
```

In the three pairs of examples just shown, one printer (Teletype Model 37) did not require **col**, and the other printer (Teletype Model 40/4) did.

Options

-c	Filter columns for output
-e	Process equations in the input file
-E	Produce equal spacing
-t	Process tables in the input file
-T_name_	Print on printer _name_
-y	Do not allow compact files
-12	Produce pica output

Formatting requests:

.P 0	Form a block paragraph
.P 1	Form an indented paragraph
.BL	Begin a bulleted list
.DL	Begin a dashed list
.ML _c_	Begin a marked list using character _c_
.RL	Begin a reference list
.VL _n_	Begin a variable-item list with space for _n_ characters
.AL _c_	Begin an autonumbered list using symbol _c_:

1	1, 2, 3, . . .
A	A, B, C, . . .
a	a, b, c, . . .
I	I, II, III, ...
i	i, ii, iii, . . .

.LI	An item in a list
.LE	End of the list

.DS	Begin a standard display
.DF	Begin a floating display
.DS I	Begin an indented display
.DS C	Begin a centered display
.DS CB	Begin a blocked, centered display
.DE	End the display
.I	Begin underlining (**nroff**) or italic (**troff**)
.B	Begin bold
.R	Roman: end underlining, italic, or bold
.SA 0	Leave right margin unjustified
.SA 1	Justify the right margin
.HU	Enter an unnumbered heading
.H *n*	Enter a numbered heading at level *n*
.SP *n*	Skip *n* blank lines
.SK	Skip a page
.OP	Skip to the next odd page
.FS	Start a footnote
*F	Use autonumbering for footnotes
.FE	End the footnote

*(DT	Enter the date
\\\\\\nP	Enter the page number
.ND	Change the date
.PH "'left'center'right'"	Change all headers
.EH "'left'center'right'"	Change even headers
.OH "'left'center'right'"	Change odd headers
.PF "'left'center'right'"	Change all footers
.EF "'left'center'right'"	Change even footers
.OF "'left'center'right'"	Change odd footers
.TC	Generate a table of contents

Note   The **mm** macro is derived from the **nroff** and **troff** commands. But **mm** is simpler to use than either of its parents.

See Also   Format text (**nroff, troff**)

Format Text

```
$ nroff [-cc] [-e] [-mc] [-np] [-op] [-sp] [-Tname] file(s)
$ troff [-cc] [-e] [-mc] [-np] [-op] [-sp] [-Tname] file(s)
```

Use **nroff** to format text for printing on a daisy-wheel printer; use **troff** for printing on a laser printer or a phototypesetter. Either command enables you to produce paragraphs, lists, displays, headings, headers, footers, footnotes, and so on. In addition, the **troff** command supports proportional spacing and font changes. The formatting commands must be embedded in the file before you enter the **nroff** or **troff** command to carry out formatting.

Application   To display formatting for file **letter** on the screen, enter **nroff letter**. If the file is very long, you can enter **nroff letter** | **page** or **nroff letter** | **more**. To format and print **letter**, enter **nroff letter** | **lp** (or **nroff letter** | **pr** | **lp**).

You can request specific pages in a number of different ways. To start at a given page (say page 11), you can enter **nroff -n11 doc** | **lp**. To print only page 11, enter **nroff -o11 doc** | **lp**.

To print pages 1-10, enter **nroff -o-10 doc** | **lp**. To print pages 11 through 15, enter **nroff -o11-15 doc** | **lp**. To print pages 11, 15, and 19, enter **nroff -o11,15,19 doc** | **lp**.

If you have to feed in sheets of paper manually, you can request a pause between pages with the **-s** option: **nroff -s doc** | **lp**.

To print on a PostScript printer, enter **troff -Tps doc** | **lp**.

Options | | |
|---|---|
| **-c**c | Select a macro package (compact version) |
| **-e** | Produce even (proportional) spacing |
| **-m**c | Select a macro package (regular version) |
| **-n**p | Start at page p |
| **-o**p | Generate the individual page (or pages) indicated |
| **-s**p | Pause every p pages |
| **-T**$name$ | Print on printer $name$: |

300	DASI 300
300S	DASI 300S
450	DASI 450
tn300	GE TermiNet 300
lp	Line printer
5510	NEC Spinwriter 5510
5520	NEC Spinwriter 5520
ps	PostScript printer
37	TeleType Model 37 (the default)

Format Text

Formatting requests:

Requests used by **nroff** *and* **troff**:

.pl *n*	Set page length to *n* lines (default 66)
.po *c*	Set page offset to *c* characters (default 0)
.ll *c*	Set line length to *c* characters (default 65)
.in *c*	Set indentation to *c* characters (default 0)
.ti *c*	Set temporary indentation to *c* characters (default 0)
.pn *n*	Set the page number to *n*
.bp	Force a page break
.ne *n*	Keep the next *n* lines together on the same page
.fi	Fill lines of text from margin to margin
.nf	Do not fill lines of text from margin to margin
.ad *c*	Adjust lines of text as indicated by *c*:

	l	Flush left
	r	Flush right
	b	Both (left and right)
	n	Same as both
	c	Centered

.na	Turn off line-adjustment
.hy	Turn on hyphenation
.nh	Turn off hyphenation
.br	Line break
.ls *n*	Set line spacing to *n*
.sp *n*	Space a line *n* lines above or below the previous line
.ce *n*	Center the next *n* lines
.ul	Underline text
.cl	Underline continuously (text and spaces)
\\%	Print the current page number
\\u	Print one-half line down (superscript)
\\d	Print one-half line down (subscript)
.*n***C**	Print in *n*-column format
.TS	Table start
.TE	Table end
.EQ	Equation start
.EN	Equation end
.de *name*	Start macro *name* (one or two characters)
..	End macro here
.*name*	Execute macro *name*

Requests used only by **troff**:

.**ps** *n*   Change point size to *n* points[1] (within a line use \f*n*)

.**vs** *n*   Change vertical spacing to *n* points

.**ss** *n*   Change word spacing to *n*/36 ems[2]

.**cs** *f n*   Change to constant character spacing of *n*/36 ems with font *f*

.**ft** *f*   Change to font *f* (within a line use \f*n*):
   R Roman
   I Italic
   B Bold
   S Special

.**fp** *n f*   Change font *f* to font position *n*

\(*xy*   Enter special character indicated by *xy*:

\(**bu**	Round bullet
\(**sq**	Square bullet
\(**em**	Em dash
\(**ru**	Baseline rule
\(**ul**	Underline
\(**co**	Copyright symbol
\(**rg**	Registered trademark symbol
\(**sc**	Section symbol
\(**dg**	Dagger
\(**dd**	Double dagger
\(**ua**	Up arrow
\(**da**	Down arrow
\(**<-**	Left arrow
\(**->**	Right arrow
\(**14**	One-quarter fraction
\(**12**	One-half fraction
\(**34**	Three-quarters fraction
\(**ct**	Cent symbol
\(**de**	Degree symbol

There are also mathematical symbols, ligatures, and the letters of the Greek alphabet in upper- and lowercase.

Notes   Use **nroff** for daisy-wheel printers (and all other printers that print with uniform spacing). Use **troff** for laser printers and phototypesetters (and all other devices that support proportional spacing).

---

[1]A *point* is a unit of measure used in typesetting, equal to 1/72 inch.

[2]An *em* is the amount of horizontal space occupied by the letter *M*.

An enhancement of **troff** called **ditroff** is the device-independent version of **troff**, which supports an unlimited number of fonts instead of just four.

See Also　Column filter (**col**)
Format equations (**eqn**, **neqn**)
Format text (**mm**)
Format tables (**tbl**)

Format Text Simply

```
$ fmt [-cs] [-w n] [file(s)]
```

Use **fmt** to provide simple formatting of files, mainly to fill text out to the right margin. The command's function is similar to that performed by the **.fi** request used by **nroff** and **troff**.

Application　To format keyboard input, enter **fmt** without options or arguments. To format file **jagged**, enter **fmt jagged**.

Options　**-c**　Crown margin mode: retain the indentation of the first two lines; align additional lines with the second

-s　Split only: do not join short lines

-w *n*　Fill to column *n* instead of the default 72

Remove Formatting Codes

```
$ deroff [-mx] [-w] [file(s)]
```

Use **deroff** to remove formatting requests for **mm**, **nroff**, and **troff**.

Application　To remove formatting requests from file **part.5**, enter **deroff part.5**.

Options　**-m**x　Delete requests from files to be formatted by a macro package:

l　Delete lists from **mm**-formatted files

m　Delete requests from **mm**-formatted files

s　Delete requests from **ms**-formatted files

-w　Build a list of words to be removed, with each word entered on a separate line

See Also　Format equations (**eqn**, **neqn**)
Format tables (**tbl**)

Format text (**mm**)
Format text (**nroff, troff**)

```
/usr/nelson/test> cat > jagged
This is a
paragraph that contains some short lines and
some long lines.  There
is no way of
knowing how long a particular line will be until you type it.  Sometimes
you have to
look at the line to determine
just how
long it will be.

/usr/nelson/test> fmt jagged
This is a paragraph that contains some short lines and some long
lines.  There is no way of knowing how long a particular line will be
until you type it.  Sometimes you have to look at the line to determine
just how long it will be.
```

An example of the fmt command

Screen Editor

```
$ vi [-ClLRx] [-ccommand] [-r[file]] [-ttag] [-wn] [+n]
[file(s)]
$ view [-ClLRx] [-ccommand] [-r[file]] [-ttag] [-wn] [+n]
[file(s)]
$ vedit [-ClLRx] [-ccommmand] [-r[file]] [-ttag] [-wn] [+n]
[file(s)]
```

Use **vi** to perform full-screen editing. You can edit just one file or a series of files in a single session. You are allowed to name a file either at the beginning or at the end of an editing session. Special features enable you to recover files lost during system malfunction, edit encrypted text, and tag locations in your files for instant recall.

A read-only mode of **vi**, called **view**, enables you to view text but not modify it. A simplified version of the editor called **vedit** is intended for beginners.

Application To begin an editing session so that you can enter new text, enter **vi**. To begin a new session with an existing file called **memo**, enter **vi memo**. To begin at the end of the file, enter **vi + memo**.

When the editing screen appears, type **a** (append text) or i (insert text) and begin entering the text. To save what you've typed, type **:w** (write). To end the session and return to the shell prompt, type **:q** (quit).

The options you can request when you begin a session are covered under Options. The commands you can use during an editing session are described under Editing Commands.

Options

-C	Begin a session with an encrypted file; enter the encryption key
-l	Begin a session with a LISP program
-L	List the names of files saved in a system failure
-R	Enter read-only mode (same as using view)
-x	Create or enter an encrypted file; enter the encryption key
-c *command*	Enter *command* in the editor
-r[*file*]	Recover *file*, which may have been lost during a system failure; entered alone, without a filename, display the names of files eligible for recovery
-t*tag*	Retrieve the file indicated at the line number specified in the **tags** file (a file that associates code names [tags] with filenames and line numbers)
-w*n*	Set the default window size to *n* lines of text
+*line*	Begin the editing session on *line* of the file; if you enter + alone, without a line number, begin editing at the end of the file (*line* can be either a number or an expression of the form /*expr*)

Editing commands:
The following commands control how and where new next is added to existing text:

A	Append text at the end of the line
a	Append text immediately following the cursor
I	Insert text at the beginning of the line
i	Insert text right in front of the cursor
O	Open a new line above the current line
o	Open a new line below the current line

Cursor movement commands:

h	Move one space to the left
j	Move one space down
k	Move one space up

l	Move one space to the right
H	Move to the top of the screen
M	Move to the middle of the screen
L	Move to the bottom of the screen
Ctrl U	Scroll up
Ctrl D	Scroll down
Ctrl B	Page back
Ctrl F	Page forward
*n***G**	Move to line *n* (last line of the file if *n* is not entered)
%	Move to the matching symbol of the pair (and), { and }, [and]

Cursor control commands that are combined with other editing commands:

b	Move to the beginning of the previous word
B	Move to the beginning of the previous word (ignore punctuation)
w	Move to the beginning of the next word
W	Move to the beginning of the next word (ignore punctuation)
e	Move to the end of the next word
E	Move to the end of the next word (ignore punctuation)
0	Move to the beginning of the line
^	Move to the first visible character of the line
$	Move to the end of the line
(	Move to the beginning of the sentence
)	Move to the end of the sentence
{	Move to the beginning of the paragraph
}	Move to the end of the paragraph
[	Move to the beginning of the section
]	Move to the end of the section

Commands combined with the cursor movement commands to change, delete, or shift text:

c*c*	Change text from the cursor to the location indicated by *c*; for example, **cw** means change from the cursor to the end of the word, and **cc** means change the entire line
d*c*	Delete text from the cursor to the location indicated by *c*; for example, **d$** means delete text from the

cursor to the end of the current line, and **dd** means delete the entire line

dnc   Delete *n* units of text as indicated by *c*; for example, **d3w** means delete three words

<c   Shift to the left the segment of text indicated by *c*; for example, **<(** means shift text from the cursor to the beginning of the sentence, and **<<** means shift the entire current line; each shift is to the preceding tab stop

<nc   Shift to the left *n* units of text as indicated by *c*; for example, **<3}** means shift three paragraphs

>c   Shift to the right the segment of text indicated by *c*; for example, **>(** means shift text from the cursor to the beginning of the sentence, and **>>** means shift the entire current line; each shift is to the preceding tab stop

>nc   Shift to the right *n* units of text as indicated by *c*; for example, **>3}** means shift three paragraphs

Search and search and replace commands:

tx   Move the cursor to the next occurrence of character *x* on the current line

fx   Find character *x* on the current line

r   Replace the character at the cursor position with another character

R   Replace a set of characters one at a time

s   Replace the character at the cursor position with a set of characters

S   Replace an entire line (same as **cc**)

/string   Search forward for *string* in the current file

?string   Search backward for *string* in the current file

*:m,n***s**/*str_1*/*str_2*/**g**   Search forward in the file, from line *m* to line *n*, substituting *str_2* for *str_1* at each occurrence

*:m,n***s**?*str_1*?*str_2*?**g**   Search backward in the file, from line *m* to line *n*, substituting *str_2* for *str_1* at each occurrence

Move or copy text commands:

To move text, you have to delete it from the current location, move the cursor to another spot, then place the text in the new location.

Moving text within the same file:

d*nc*   Delete text from the current location
       Move to the target location

P   Place the text above the current line or before the
       current character

p   Place the text below the current line or after the
       current character

Moving text between files:

"*x*d*nc*   Delete text from the current location in the
          source file to buffer *x* (a-z)
          Move to the target file and location

"*x***P**   Place the text from buffer *x* above the current
          line or before the current character in the target
          file

"*x***p**   Place the text from buffer *x* below the current
          line or after the current character in the target
          file

To copy text, you have to "yank" it (make a copy of it)
from the current location, place the cursor in another
spot, then place the text in the new location.

Copying text within the same file:

y*nc*   Yank text from the current location
       Move to the target location

P   Place the text above the current line or before the
       current character

p   Place the text below the current line or after the
       current character

Copying text between files:

"*xync*   Yank text from the current location in the source
         file to buffer *x* (a-z)
         Move to the target file and location

"*x***P**   Place the text from buffer *x* above the current
          line or before the current character in the target
          file

"*x***p**   Place the text from buffer *x* below the current
          line or after the current character in the target
          file

Commands to set a vi option or abbreviation, or map a key:

:set *option*   Set the option indicated (enter **:set all** for a
                  list of available options)

:ab *abc expression*	Assign *expression* to *abc*
:map *key command*	Assign *command* to *key* (the keys available include the function keys and g K k q V v ; _ = *)

Exit commands:

:wq	Write and quit this editing session
:x	Conditional write and quit (same as ZZ)
:q!	Abandon the text changes

Note   The UNIX system also has a line editor called **ed**, but it is much too difficult for the average person to use.

See Also   Encrypt text (**crypt**)

6

Printing

Chapter 5 discussed the commands you use to edit and format text. This chapter covers the commands you use to print a document or to prepare a document for printing.

Accept Printing Requests

```
$ accept name
```

Use **accept** to accept printing requests to printer *name*.

Application To accept printing requests to printer **LJ3**, enter **accept LJ3**.

Note Use **reject** and **accept** to control the queueing of print jobs. Use **disable** and **enable** to control the flow of jobs from the queue to the target printer.

See Also Reject printing requests (**reject**)

Cancel Printing Requests

```
$ cancel [request-id] [printer]
$ cancel [-u user-id] [printer]
```

Use **cancel** to remove a file from the printing queue, using the request-id provided by the system. You can also stop a printing job that has already begun.

Application Each time you initiate a printing job with the **lp** command, the system returns a request-id. You can also display a list of request-ids when you run the **lpstat** command. Each request-id gives the name of the target printer, followed by a hyphen and a sequence number (for example, mx80-2409).

To remove the printing job identified as mx80-2409, enter
cancel mx80-2409. To remove the current printing job
running on printer mx80, enter **cancel mx80**. If your
login name is **quinn**, you can cancel all your own
printing requests by entering **cancel quinn**.

Options   *request-id*   Stop the printing job identified by the
                               system as *request-id*

          -u *user-id*   Stop any printing job initiated by the user
                               identified (name or ID)

Note   If your file is currently in the print queue, **cancel**
            removes it. If the file is already being printed, **cancel**
            stops it and begins the next job in the queue.

See Also   Display printer status (**lpstat**)
                Print a file (**lp**)

Configure the Spooling System

```
$ lpadmin [-pprinter [-cname] -vdevice [- mmodel | -eprinter |
-icustom]]  [-x] [-o  stty=list] [-T type] [- M] [-f
[allow:]name] [-S list]
```

Use **lpadmin** to assign a printer interface program to a printer, identify
the type of device, designate a default printer for the system, allow and
mount forms, and mount character sets and print wheels.

A printer interface program is a C program (or a shell script) that
collects information from each **lp** command line and passes it to the
printer for printing. The program typically prints a banner page with
the user's name, the date and time, and any title requested; checks for
the number of copies requested; and sets up a loop to handle printing of
more than one file.

Application   First turn off the print spooling system by entering
                   lpshut. Then, to assign to printer **LJ2** device file **/dev/
                   tty08** and the same interface used by printer **LJ1**, enter
                   lpadmin -p LJ2 -v/dev/tty08 -e LJ1. Follow with **accept
                   LJ2, enable LJ2**, and **lpsched** to activate the printer and
                   turn the print spooling system back on.

                   To make this same printer the default destination for the
                   system, enter **lpadmin -d LJ2**.

To remove printer **mx80** from the system, enter **lpadmin -x mx80**.

Options	-p*printer*	Name of the printer
	-c*name*	Assign a printer to class *name*
	-v*device*	Device name for the printer, followed by one of the following:

	-m*model*	Use a model printer interface program provided by **lp**
	-e*printer*	Use the printer interface program used by existing printer *printer*
	-i*custom*	Use a custom printer interface program called *custom*

-o stty=*list*	Change specifications for the printer named
-T *name*	Specify printer type *name*, which is found in the **terminfo** directory
-M	Mount a printed form (with -**f** *name*); unmount a printer (with -**f none**)
-f [**allow:**]*name*	Allow (if **allow:** is included) or mount form *name*; unmount a printer if *name* is **none**
-S *list*	Mount the character set or print wheel named

Note   You can use **lpadmin** for a variety of tasks when you set up a printing subsystem or when you add a new printer to it.

See Also   Accept printing requests (**accept**)
Cancel printing requests (**cancel**)
Disable a printer (**disable**)
Enable a printer (**enable**)
Display printer status (**lpstat**)
Reject printing requests (**reject**)

Disable a Printer

```
$ disable [-cW] [-r"reason"] name
```

Use **disable** to disable printer *name*.

Application To disable printer **LJ3**, enter **disable LJ3**. To disable it only after all current jobs have completed and to give an explanation to users, enter **disable -r"Adding toner" -W LJ3**.

Options   -c   Cancel any printing jobs currently in progress
          -r"*reason*"   Reason for disabling the printer
          -W   Wait for jobs currently in progress to complete

Note   Use **reject** and **accept** when you have to take a printer off-line for any period of time. For briefer interruptions, use **disable** and **enable**.

See Also Enable a printer (**enable**)

Display Printer Status

```
$ lpstat [options]
```

Use **lpstat** to display information about the status of printers and printing requests on the system.

Application The **lpstat** command is useful to both ordinary users and system administrators. An ordinary user can obtain information about the status of current printing requests by entering **lpstat**.

A system administrator can obtain much more comprehensive information about the overall setup and status of printers by entering **lpstat -t**. This command tells you the default printer on the system, the members of each class of printers, which printers are currently accepting jobs, and which printers are idle.

Options   -a [*list*]   Display the acceptance status of all classes and printers (or all those listed)

-c [*list*]	Display the names of all classes and all printers that belong to each class (or those classes listed)
-d	Display the name of the default destination printer
-f [*list*] [-D] [-l]	Display which forms the system recognizes (or verify those listed): -l List descriptions of forms
-o [*list*]	Display the status of all output printer requests (or for those classes, printers, and request-ids listed)
-p [*list*] [-D] [-l]	Display the status of all printers (or of those listed by name): -D List printer descriptions -l Show full descriptions for local printers
-r	Display information about **lpsched**, the **lp** scheduler
-R	Display the position of a job in the queue
-S [*list*] [-l]	Display all character sets and daisy wheels supported (or verifies those named): -l List printers that support each character set or daisy wheel
-t	Total: display all information in one report
-u [*list*]	Display printing status for all users (or users listed by name)
-v [*list*]	Display pathnames of devices for all printers (or printers listed by name)

Note   If you want to cancel a printing request and you don't remember the request-id of the job, you can use **lpstat** to find out. If you're a system administrator and you don't remember which printers belong to which classes and which printers are currently idle, you can find out with **lpstat**.

See Also   Cancel printing requests (**cancel**)
Print files (**lp**)
Configure the spooling system (**lpadmin**)

Enable a Printer

```
$ enable name
```

Use **enable** to enable printer *name*.

Application To enable printer **LJ3**, enter **enable LJ3**.

Option Use **reject** and **accept** when you have to take a printer off-line for any period of time. For briefer interruptions, use **disable** and **enable**.

See Also Enable a printer (**enable**)

Move Jobs to Another Printer

```
$ lpmove list printer
```

If a printer stops working or if the queue for one printer gets too long, you can use **lpmove** to move some of the printing jobs to another printer of the same type.

Application To move the printing jobs with request-ids LJ2-114, LJ2-115, and LJ2-116 from LJ2 to LJ3, enter **lpmove LJ2-114 LJ2-115 LJ2-116 LJ3**.

Note The printer to which you move the jobs must be compatible with the printer for which they were originally destined. For example, you can move jobs for a dot-matrix printer only to another dot-matrix printer or jobs for a daisy-wheel printer only to another daisy-wheel printer.

See Also Accept printing requests (**accept**)
Disable a printer (**disable**)
Enable a printer (**enable**)
Reject printing requests (**reject**)

Prepare Files for Printing

```
$ pr [-adfFmprt] [-eincn] [-h header] [-1n] [+p] [-col] [-on]
[-sc] [-wn] [file(s)]
```

Use **pr** to prepare files for displaying or printing. In its default mode, **pr** breaks text into pages and inserts a heading at the top of each. It can generate output in any number of columns you specify up to the limit for your terminal.

Application To prepare file **secret** for screen display, enter **pr secret**. If **secret** is a long document, you can enter **pr secret | page** or **pr secret | more**. To prepare **secret** for printing, enter **pr secret | lp**.

To display a text file in three-column format, enter **pr -3 secret**. To print the text in three columns, enter **pr -3 secret | lp**.

To merge three files across the screen, enter **pr -m secret codes ltrs**. To print the merged files, enter **pr -m secret codes ltrs | lp**. The output will be similar to that produced by the **paste** command, except that **pr** will generate three separate columns, while **paste** will simply separate the three with tabs.

Options

+n	Begin printing on page *n* (default 1)
-n	Generate *n* columns of output (default 1); incompatible with **-m** option)
-a	Print multicolumn output across instead of down
-d	Double-space the output
-ecn	Expand input character *c* to each *n*th position (by default, *c* is **tab** and *n* is 8, implying positions 1, 9, 17, . . .)
-f	Use formfeed to begin a new page; pause for **Return** before the first page of output
-F	Fold input lines to fit the line width
-h *header*	Replace the filename with *header* as the page header
-icn	Convert input spaces to character *c* every *n*th position (by default, *c* is **tab** and *n* is 8)
-1n	Set the page length to *n* lines (default 66)

-m	Merge input files, placing each in its own column; incompatible with *-n* option
-n*cn*	Number the output lines, allowing *n* spaces for line numbers and separating numbers from text with *c* (by default, *c* is **tab** and *n* is 5)
-o*n*	Offset each line by *n* positions (default 0)
-p	Pause between pages for screen output
-r	Suppress messages if **pr** fails to open one of the input files
-s*c*	Use *c* to separate columns of output (default **tab**)
-t	Suppress headers and trailers; ignore **-h**
-w*n*	Set line width of the output to *n* characters (default 72); applies only to **-n** and **-m** options)

Note In the absence of any options, **pr** divides its output into pages. Each page includes a 5-line header, a 56-line body, and a 5-line footer. The third line of the header contains the date, time, filename, and page number; all other header and footer lines are blank.

See Also Concatenate files (**cat**)
Concatenate files horizontally (**paste**)
Display large files (**more**, **page**)
Display large files (**pg**)

Print Files

```
$ lp [options] file(s)
```

Use **lp** to queue a file or a set of files for printing on one of the system's printers. You can request a particular printer or a class of printers. You can also request multiple copies, special handling of your print job, and notification upon completion.

Application To place file **memo** in the print queue, enter **lp memo**. The print scheduler will direct the file to a printer and return a request-id, which will be displayed below your command line.

You can also queue a set of files, as shown here: **lp ch.3 ch.4 ch.5.**

The **lp** command can also accept files processed by other commands. For example, **pr -2 secret I lp**. In this example, **lp** accepts text in two-column format from the **pr** command.

To sort text in file **data**, format it, and print it, enter **sort data I pr I lp**.

You can also use a number of options with **lp**. To print three copies of **doc**, enter **lp -n3 doc**. To have an electronic mail message sent to you upon completion of your printing job, enter **lp -m doc**.
To print five copies of **secret** in three-column format, with a message on completion, enter **pr -3 secret I lp -m -n5**.

Options			
-c		Copy files instead of linking them to the directory	
-d*printer*		Request printing on *printer* instead of the default printer	
-f*form* [**-d any**]		Print on form *form*, using any printer that supports the form if **-d any** is included	
-H*special*:			
	hold	Hold the printing request (or suspend a printing job already in progress)	
	immediate	Begin printing immediately after completion of the current printing job	
	resume	Resume printing on a job being held	
-m		Notify user by mail on completion	
-n*n*		Print *n* copies (default 1)	
-o*option*		Specify options for class or printer:	
	cpi=*n*	Print *n* characters per inch; or	
	elite	12 characters per inch	
	pica	10 characters per inch	
	compressed	As many as possible	
	length=*n*	Specify page length:	
		*n***c**	*n* centimeters
		*n***i**	*n* inches
		n	*n* lines

lpi=_n_	Print _n_ lines per inch
nobanner	Omit the banner page
nofilebreak	Omit the formfeed between files
stty=_options_	Options for the **stty** command
width=_n_	Specify page width:
	_n_**c** _n_ centimeters
	_n_**i** _n_ inches
	_n_ _n_ lines
-P_list_	Print the pages listed
-q_level_	Assign a priority level from 0 to 39 (0 is highest)
-s	Suppress messages from **lp**
-S_chset_ [**-d any**]	Use the character set (or print wheel) named, using any printer that supports it if **-d any** is included
-t_title_	Print _title_ on the banner page
-T_type_ [**-r**]	Print on a printer that supports content type _type_, using a filter if necessary if **-r** is included
-w	Notify on completion by writing to the user's terminal
-y_list_	Print according to the modes listed

Notes

Unless the appropriate printer is already available, your printing request is placed in a queue, where it awaits processing by a _daemon_ called **lpsched**. The **lpsched** process returns a message of the form, "request id is _printer-number_ (_n_ file(s))," where _printer_ is the name of the printer, _number_ is a sequence number, and _n_ is the number of files you have queued for printing in this request.

To monitor the progress of your printing requests, you can use the **lpstat** command, which also uses request ids. If it becomes necessary to cancel a printing request, you can use the **cancel** command with the request id (that is, **cancel** _printer-number_).

See Also

Cancel printing requests (**cancel**)
Disable printers (**disable**)
Display printer status (**lpstat**)

Reject Printing Requests

```
$ reject name
```

Use **reject** to reject printing requests to printer *name*.

Application To reject printing requests to printer **LJ3**, enter **reject LJ3**.

Note Use **reject** and **accept** when you have to take a printer off-line for any period of time. For briefer interruptions, use **disable** and **enable**.

See Also Accept printing requests (**accept**)

Turn the Print Spooler On

```
$ lpsched
```

Use **lpsched** to turn the print spooler on.

Application You can enter **lpsched** at the command line. But the best way to use the command is to place it in the **rc** file. Then the print spooler will start when the system starts.

Note The **lpsched** command starts a *daemon*, a background process that runs on its own.

See Also Turn the print spooler off (**lpshut**)

7

Communication

This chapter covers the commands that enable you to communicate with users either on your own system or on other systems.

Call Terminal

```
$ ct [-hv] [-sspeed] [-wm] [-xn] system
```

Use **ct** to call another terminal and log into a UNIX system.

Application To dial into a terminal through phone number 555-4800 at 9600 bits per second, enter **ct -s9600 5554800**. You can also use a network name to reach the other system, as shown in this example: **ct -s9600 minerva**.

Options
-h	Prevent hangup
-v	Output status information to standard error
-sspeed	Set transmission rate to speed bits per second
-wm	Wait m minutes for the line
-xn	Level n for debugging
system	Telephone number or system name

Note If a connection takes place, **ct** automatically logs you into the host system via the target terminal.

See Also Call up another system (**cu**)

Call Up Another System

```
$ cu [-dehmnot] [-bn] [-ctype] [-lport] [-sspeed] system
```

Use **cu** to call up another system. The other system can be another terminal, another UNIX system, or a non-UNIX system.

Application To call a system whose phone number is 555-3600 and communicate at 2400 bits per second, enter **cu -s2400 5553600**. The speed option (**-s**) enables you to set the data rate.

Suppose you have to dial 9 for an outside line, dial 1 and then area code 213, and then, when you reach the desired number, you have to dial an extension, say 273. Then you could enter **cu -s2400 9=12135553600-273**. The equal sign (=) allows you to wait for another dial tone, while the minus sign (-) allows you a four-second pause.

You can also call another UNIX system on the **uucp** network to which your system is connected. To display a list of such systems, enter the **uuname** command. Suppose the name **hercules** appears on this list. Then you can call **hercules** without direct dialing, as shown here: **cu -s2400 hercules**.

Whether you access the other system by number or by network name, you can keep a record of your **cu** session by using the **tee** command. While you make the initial connection, include **tee** on your command line, as shown here: **cu -s2400 hercules | tee session**. Everything will be stored in file **session** in the current directory. You will have a complete record of the entire session.

If you are calling another UNIX system and you have a user account on it, a login prompt will appear and you can log into the system.

Once you've made a connection, you can use a number of on-line commands to interact with the other system. You can send a file (say, **findings**) to any other system, UNIX or non-UNIX, by entering **~> findings**.

If your system is connected to another UNIX system and you have the necessary permissions, you can send the same file by entering **~%put findings**. You can also copy a file (say, **results**) from the remote system to your own by entering **~%take results**. The file will be stored in your current directory.

When you want to end your remote session, press **Ctrl D** to log out. When the login: prompt appears, enter **~.** to end the session.

Options   -d   Display diagnostics
-e   Set even parity
-h   Half-duplex

-m	Use modem control
-n	Prompt for a telephone number
-o	Set odd parity
-t	Call an ASCII terminal
-b*n*	Set character size to *n* bits
-c*type*	Use only *type* to match a device
-l*port*	Dial into a terminal port
-s*speed*	Set the transmission rate to *speed* bit/s
system	You can reach the target system by entering a phone number, a system name, or a local area network (LAN) address. For phone numbers, you can embed the following:
	- Four-second delay
	= Wait for another dial tone

On-line commands:
Once you are connected to the other system and logged in, you can use a set of commands to perform specific functions:

~!*cmd*	Run command *cmd* on the local system
~$*cmd*	Run command *cmd* on the local system and send the output to the target system
~%cd *dir*	Change to directory *dir* on the local system
~%put *file*	Copy file *file* from the local system to the target system
~%take *file*	Copy file *file* from the target system to the local system
~!	Exit from **cu** to the local shell
~.	Disconnect the local system from the target system
~?	Display a list of all on-line commands

Note
Although its esoteric on-line commands are difficult to use, the **cu** command can get you connected to almost any computer, device, or network node on the map. If it has a modem and a phone number, **cu** can reach it. You can use **cu** to check for a connection before starting up a sophisticated communication program like **uucp**.

See Also
Call terminal (**ct**)
Redirect and display output (**tee**)
UNIX-to-UNIX copy (**uucp**)

Carry on a Dialog

```
$ talk user[@host] [terminal]
```

Use **talk** to carry on a dialog with a user on another terminal.

Application To begin a dialog with user **ned**, enter **talk ned**. If **ned** uses more than one terminal, you can select one of the two by entering a command line like this: **talk ned /dev/ tty12**.

If you succeed in reaching the other user, both of your screens will be split into vertical halves. Your input will appear on the upper half of your own screen and the lower half of the other user's screen. The other user's input will appear on the upper half of the remote screen and the lower half of your screen.

Options
user   Call *user*
host   Name of remote system *user* is logged into
terminal Direct call to the terminal with device address *terminal*

Notes You can reach a user either on your own system or on another. As long as the other user hasn't disallowed messages with the **mesg** command, you should be able to start a dialog. Some programs like **pr** and **vi** also disallow messages.

Using **talk** can be easier than sending a series of **write** messages back and forth.

See Also Send a message to another terminal (**write**)
Send and receive mail (**mail**)
Set terminal access (**mesg**)

Compute Checksum and Block Count

```
$ sum [-r] file(s)
```

Use **sum** to compute a checksum and a block count for a file.

Application To compute a checksum on a file called **count**, enter **sum count**. The checksum and a block count will appear on a line.

Option   -r   Use an alternate algorithm to compute the checksum

Note   A checksum, like a parity check, is a simple method for comparing a file before and after copying or transmission. A checksum is the sum of the numerical value of all the characters in the file (or a similar calculation).

See Also   Count lines, words, and characters (**wc**\, Chapter 3)

Connect to Remote Using TELNET Protocol

```
$ telnet system [port]
```

Use **telnet** to log into a remote system, UNIX or non-UNIX, usually over a network.

Application   To connect to a system called **homer**, enter **telnet homer**. You can log in in terminal mode. Use the escape character, which is ^] by default, to toggle between terminal mode and command mode.

In command mode, you can use a number of commands. Use one of two commands, **close** or **quit**, to end the session.

Options   *system*   Either the name of the remote host or its network address

port   Optional port identification

On-line commands:
? [*cmd*]   Display a summary of on-line commands; if *cmd* is included, display help for the command

close   Close the session and exit

display [*value(s)*]   Display all **set** and **toggle** values; display the value(s) named

mode *mode*   *Change to mode:*
    character   Character mode
    line   Line mode

open *system* [*port*]   Open connection to *system*

quit   Close session and exit (same as **close**)

send *char(s)*	*Send special characters to the target system:*	
	?	Display help for **send**
	ao	Abort output
	ayt	Are you there?
	brk	Break
	ec	Erase character
	el	Erase line
	escape	Escape
	ga	Go ahead
	ip	Interrupt process
	nop	No operation
	synch	Synch (discard unused input)
set *value*	*Set a value:*	
	echo	Toggle local echo on or off
	eof	End-of-file for remote system
	erase	Erase character
	escape	Escape character (default ^])
	flushoutput	Flush output
	interrupt	Interrupt process
	kill	Erase line
	quit	Break
status	Display status	
toggle *value(s)*	*Toggle values:*	
	?	Display **toggle** settings
	autoflush	Send interrupt or quit to the remote system (default is whatever is set by **stty**)
	autosynch	Synch after **interrupt** or **quit** (default off)
	crmod	Convert **CR** to **CR LF** (default no conversion)
	debug	Toggle debugging on or off (default off)
	localchars	Convert local commands into remote control (default on for line mode, off for character mode)

netdata	Toggle hexadecimal display of network data (default off)
options	Toggle display of protocol processing (default off)
z	In job control shell, suspend **telnet**

Note   To access another UNIX system, you can use either **telnet** or **rlogin**.

See Also   Remote login (**rlogin**)

Display News Items

```
$ news [-ans] [items]
```

Use **news** to display news items on the local system, which are stored in /usr/news.

Application   To display the most recent news items, enter **news**. To display all news items on the system, enter **news -a**.

To display names only, enter **news -n**. To display only the number of news items, enter **news -s**.

Options

-a	Display all items
-n	Display names, but not contents, of all current items
-s	Display the number of current items
items	Names of files in /usr/news with news

Notes   News items are stored in separate files in /usr/news. Each time you run **news**, the program checks for the last time you ran the program and displays only those items stored since that time.

Press **Del** once to halt display of a news item, twice to halt and exit from the program.

See Also   Look at USENET bulletin board (**readnews**)

File Transfer Protocol

```
$ ftp [-dgintv] [system]
```

Use **ftp** to log into another UNIX system on the Internet network and copy files to or from the other system. Once the program has logged you in, you can copy either text or program files, depending on your current mode (ASCII or binary).

Application To make a connection to another system (say, **hercules**), enter **ftp hercules**. If you have an account on the system, you can log in and carry out a number of different transactions. To keep a record of your remote session, enter **ftp hercules | tee session**.

Once you've made a connection, you can use a number of on-line commands. To display a list of available commands, enter **help** or **?**. You can also display help for a particular command. For example, you can enter **help get** or **? get**.

To send a file called **findings** to the remote system, enter **put findings**. To check the current directory on the remote system, enter **pwd** (just as you would on your own system).

To copy a file from the remote system to your own, enter **get results**. To change to another directory (say, **plans** in the same parent), enter **cd ../plans**.

When the session is over, enter **quit**, **close**, or **bye**. You will return to the shell prompt.

Options

-d	Enable debugging
-g	Disable expansion of filenames
-i	Disable interactive prompts
-n	Enable automatic login
-t	Enable tracing of packets
-v	Display responses from target system
system	Either a name or a network address (four numbers separated by periods)

On-line commands:

! [*cmd*]	Run a shell (or command *cmd*)
$ *macro* [*arg(s)*]	Run *macro* with optional argument(s)
account [*password*]	Set an additional password
? [*cmd*]	Display command summary; display help for command *cmd*
append *file_1* [*file_2*]	Append local file *file_1* to remote file *file_2*
ascii	Use network ASCII representation of characters
bell	Follow each file transfer with the sound of the beeper (bell)
binary	Use image representation of characters
bye	End session and exit from the program
case	Toggle case mapping on or off (the default)
cd *dir*	Change to directory *dir* on the remote system
cdup	Move up to the parent directory on the target system
close	End session and return to the shell prompt
cr	Toggle stripping of carriage returns
delete *file*	Delete *file* on the target system
debug	Toggle debugging on or off (the default)
dir [*dir*] [*file*]	Display the contents of *dir* on the target system; if local file *file* is included, store the output in *file*
disconnect	End session and return to the shell prompt
form [*fmt*]	Set carriage control format to *fmt*
get *file_1* [*file_2*]	Retrieve file *file_1* on the remote system; store in local file *file_2*
glob	Toggle expansion of filenames
hash	Toggle a number display for each block transferred

help [*cmd*]	Display a summary of commands; display help for any command *cmd* named
lcd [*dir*]	Change directory to *dir* (or to **$HOME** by default) on your local system
ls [*dir*] [*file*]	Display contents of directory *dir* on remote system (default current directory); store in *file* (default your screen)
macdef *macro*	Enter macro definition at your keyboard, terminated by a blank line; store definition in file *macro*
mdelete [*file(s)*]	Delete the files named on the remote system
mdir *rfiles lfiles*	Multifile **dir**
mget *file(s)*	Multifile **get**: retrieve files from the remote system
mkdir *dir*	Create (make) a directory on the remote system
mls *rfile(s) lfile*	Multifile **ls**
mode [**stream**]	Change to **stream** mode of transfer
mput *lfiles*	Multifile **put** for files indicated
nmap [*file_1 file_2*]	Map filename *file_1* to *file_2*; remove mapping if no files are named
ntrans [*infile* [*outfile*]]	Translate by characters; end translation if no files are named [***]
open *system* [*port*]	Connect to *system* (optional *port* may also be included)
prompt	Toggle prompting on or off
proxy *cmd*	Run **ftp** command *cmd* on a secondary connection
put *lfile* [*rfile*]	Copy (**put**) local file *lfile* on the remote system, using the same name unless another (*rfile*) is named
pwd	Display ("print") the name of the working directory on the remote system

quit	End session and exit from the program
quote *arguments*	Transfer *arguments* to the remote system
recv *file_1* [*file_2*]	Retrieve file *file_1* on the remote system; store in local file *file_2* (same as **get**)
remotehelp [*cmd*]	Display help from the remote system
rename *file_1 file_2*	Rename *file_1* on the remote system *file_2*
reset	Reset
rmdir *dir*	Remove directory *dir* on the remote system
runique	Toggle unique filename mapping on your local system
send *lfile* [*rfile*]	Copy local file *lfile* on the remote system, using the same name unless another (*rfile*) is named (same as **put**)
status	Display the status of **ftp**
struct [*file*]	Set file structure
sunique	Toggle unique filename mapping on the remote system
tenex	Set up for TENEX systems
trace	Toggle packet tracing on or off
type [*type*]	Set type for representation: **ascii** (the default) **binary** **image**
user [*password*] [*account*]	Log into the remote system
verbose	Toggle verbose mode on or off

Notes   If you don't enter a system name on the command line, **ftp** will prompt you for one. You can enter either a system name or a network address.

Many sites accept a login of **anonymous** for public **ftp** access.

See Also   Remote copy (**rcp**)
Remote login (**rlogin**)

Remote Copy

```
$ rcp [-p] file_1 file_2$ rcp [-pr] file(s) dir
```

Use **rcp** to copy files to and from another system.

Application To copy a file called **plans** in your home directory to directory **/u1/ts/jared** on another system called **venus**, enter **rcp plans venus:/u1/ts/jared**. You must have permission to write to the target directory.

If you want to try to retain the file's permissions and time-stamps, use the **-p** option, as shown here: **rcp -p plans venus:/u1/ts/jared**.

To copy a file called **secret** in directory **/u1/ts/jared** along with the contents of all subdirectories into your home directory, enter **rcp -r venus:/u1/ts/jared/secret**.

Options **-p** Preserve permissions and timestamps for files copied

  -r Recursively copy each subdirectory under the path named

Note You can use **ftp**, **rcp**, or **uucp** to copy files, depending on which is available and works best at your installation.

See Also File transfer protocol (**ftp**)
Send and receive mail (**mailx**)
UNIX-to-UNIX copy (**uucp**)

Remote Login

```
$ rlogin [-8] [-e c] [-1 user] system
```

Use **rlogin** to log into another system and carry out a session.

Application To log into a system called **ranger**, enter **rlogin ranger**. If you have an account on the remote system, you will be allowed to execute commands on that system.

To log in as another user named **jud**, enter **rlogin -1 jud ranger**.

You can end the remote session with either **exit** or **Ctrl D**.

Options -8 Use 8-bit words

-**e** *c* Change the escape character from the default ~
to *c*

-**l** *user* Log in as *user*

Note While you are logged into the remote system, your local session will be suspended and all commands you enter will be run on the remote system. You can use **rlogin** and **rcp** together.

See Also Call up another system (**cu**)
Remote copy (**rcp**)
UNIX-to-UNIX copy (**uucp**)

Send and Receive Mail

```
$ mailx [options] user(s)
```

Use **mailx** to send electronic mail to another user or group of users, or to receive electronic mail from other users. The **mailx** command supersedes an older **mail** command used in earlier releases of UNIX.

Application To send a message to user **wilma**, enter **mailx wilma**. The command will then prompt you for a "Subject: " and for the text of your message, which you terminate with **Ctrl D**.

You can also redirect the message from a text file already stored. For example, suppose you have a message stored in a file called **meeting**. To send this message to user **wilma**, enter **mailx wilma < meeting**.

Options *For sending:*

-**d** Display debugging results

-**F** File the message in a file named after the first user to receive the message

-**h** *n* Set the number of network hops to *n*

-**i** Ignore interrupt signals

-**n** Ignore the default initialization file **/usr/lib/mailx/mailx.rc**

-**r** *address* Pass *address* to network delivery software

-**s** *subject* Set "Subject: " to *subject*; avoid the prompt

-**U** Convert a **uucp** address to an Internet address

-**V** Display the version of **mailx**

For receiving:

-e   Check for incoming mail: 1 means mail; 0 means no mail

-f [*file*] Store your mail in *file* instead of **/usr/mail**/*user* (if you don't include a name, **mbox** is used by default)

-H   Headers: display only header summary, not text

-I   Display group and id header lines, along with the regular header lines

-n   Ignore the default initialization file **/usr/lib/mailx/mailx.rc**

-N   Suppress display of header summary

-T *file* Store header lines in *file*

-u *user* Read another user's mail (if you have permission)

-V   Display the version of **mailx**

Header contents:

Each header line contains the following information about one incoming message:

Status code One of the following:

D	Deleted
N	New
O	Old
R	Read
U	Unread
>	Pointer to the current message

Date	Postmark
From	Sender
To	Recipient(s)
Subject	Subject
Cc	User(s) copied
Bcc	User(s) blind copied

Escape commands:

You can use any of the following commands while you are typing your outgoing message:

~?	Help: display a list of escape commands
~s *title*	Subject: add or change "Subject:"
~t *user(s)*	To: add more names of addressees
~c *user(s)*	Copy: add names to the "cc:" list
~h	Subject/To/Copy: add or change all three

~v	Edit your message with **vi**
~r *file*	Read *file* into your message
~w *file*	Write your message to *file*
~p	Display ("print") your message
~f *list*	Forward the messages listed
~m *list*	Forward the messages listed, indented
~! *command*	Run UNIX command (**Ctrl D** to return to **mailx**)
~| *command*	Pipe your message to a UNIX command; use the output in place of your current message
~.	Terminate your message (same as **Ctrl D**)
~A	Insert signature message **Sign** into your message
~a	Insert alternate signature message **sign**
~q	Quit: save your message and exit from **mailx**
~x	Exit from **mailx** without saving your message

Response commands:

You can use any of the following commands (short or long versions) while reading incoming mail:

?		Help: display commands and functions
=		Display the current message number
l	**list**	Partial help: display commands only
	headers [*list*]	Display headers for messages listed
z[+]		Scroll forward through headers
z-		Scroll back through headers
f	**from** [*list*]	Display header information for the messages listed
to	**top** [*list*]	Display the first five lines of the messages listed
n	**next** [*msg*]	Go to the next message that matches *msg*
p	**print** [*list*]	Display ("print") each message listed
	type [*list*]	Same as **print**

	Type [*list*]	Same as **print**
ho	**hold** [*list*]	Hold messages in your mailbox (/**usr mail**/*user*)
pre	**preserve** [*list*]	Same as **hold**
s	**save** [*list*] [*file*]	Save message(s) in *file* (by default, your mailbox)
d	**delete** [*list*]	Delete message(s)
u	**undelete** [*list*]	Restore message(s) deleted during the current session
e	**edit** [*list*]	Edit message(s), using the editor assigned to the EDITOR variable (default **ed**)
R	**Reply** [*list*]	Reply to sender only
r	**reply** [*list*]	Reply to sender and also other recipients
	Respond [*list*]	Same as **Reply**
	respond [*list*]	Same as **reply**
cd [*dir*]		Change to directory *dir* (default **$HOME**)
!*command*		Execute UNIX *command*, then return to **mailx**
ex	**exit**	Exit from **mailx** without saving
x	**xit**	Same as **exit**
q	**quit**	Quit **mailx**; save messages

Notes

The **mailx** command works under the control of three shell variables (HOME, MAIL, MAILRC) and over 40 **mailx** variables (including EDITOR, LISTER, and MBOX). Some of the **mailx** variables, such as EDITOR, are well worth setting; others are less important. The place to set them permanently is $HOME/**mailrc**.

The **mailx** command also has quite a few more commands. But at some point you have to ask yourself the question, "How important is it to become a power user on the mail system?"

See Also

Carry on a dialog (**talk**)
Connect to remote using TELNET protocol (**telnet**)
UNIX-to-UNIX copy (**uucp**)
Write to another user (**write**)

Set Terminal Access

```
$ mesg [-y][-n]
```

Use this command to grant or deny permission to other users to access your terminal using either the **talk** or the **write** command.

Application Use one of the two arguments for **mesg** as follows:

-**y** Yes: allow other users to send you messages (the default)

-**n** No: prevent other users from sending you messages

Enter the **mesg** command without an argument to display a code that indicates the current status of your terminal:

0 Messages are allowed (**-y**)

1 Messages are not allowed (**-n**)

2 The **mesg** command failed to execute because of an error

Note This command allows you to work at your terminal without interruption. With some commands, like **vi**, messages are prohibited automatically without **mesg**.

See Also Carry on a dialog (**talk**)
Send a message (**write**)

UNIX-to-UNIX Copy

```
$ uucp [-cCdfjmr] [-gp] [-nuser] [-sfile] [-xn] file(s)
target
```

The **uucp** is just one of a suite of commands that enable you to work between UNIX systems. However, **uucp** is often the name used to describe all the commands collectively, as well as the network across which they operate. The **uucp** network supports three main activities:

1. The use of **mailx** to send electronic messages between different systems on the network.

2. The use of the **uucp** command to copy files from one system to another.

3. The use of the **uux** command to run commands on another system.

Application   To copy file report to directory **/usr/spool/uucppublic** on system **zeus**, enter **uucp report zeus!/usr/spool/ uucppublic** or **uucp report zeus!~/**.

To receive notification once the file has been copied, use the **-m** option, as shown here: **uucp -m report zeus!~/**.

The **uucp** command, like the **cp** command, supports wildcard characters, as in this example: **uucp ltr.* zeus!~/**.

Options

-c	Copy the actual *file(s)* (default)
-C	Copy *file(s)* to a spooling directory en route to the ultimate destination
-d	Create any directories that may be needed (default)
-f	Do not create directories that do not already exist
-g*p*	Set job priority to *p*
-j	Display job identifier
-m	Notify sender by mail upon completion
-n*user*	Notifier *user* on the remote system upon completion
-r	Queue *file(s)*, but don't transfer them
-s*file*	Show status in *file* (full pathname)
-x*n*	Set debugging level *n*
p	Job priority (number or letter); lower number or letter indicates higher priority
n	Debug level: 0-9; 0 for least information, 9 for most
target	Optional system name and exclamation point (bang!), followed by a full pathname (e.g., **zeus!/ usr/spool/uucppublic**)

Notes   To promote system security, system administrators often designate **/usr/spool/uucppublic** as the starting point for outgoing files and the destination for incoming files.

The reason for requesting notification by mail is that transmission over the **uucp** network is often very slow. It may take a day or longer for your files to reach their destination.

See Also   Call up another system (**cu**)
Remote login (**rlogin**)

Remote copy (**rcp**)
Send or receive mail (**mailx**)
UNIX-to-UNIX execute (**uux**)
UNIX-to-UNIX status (**uustat**)

UNIX-to-UNIX Execute

```
$ uux [-] [-bcCjnprz] [-auser] [-gp] [-sfile] [-xn] command
```

Use **uux** to execute a UNIX command on another UNIX system.

Application Suppose several systems on a **uucp** network share a laser printer, which is on system **zeus**. To print file **report** on the laser printer on the other system, enter **cat report |
uux -zeus!lp -dlaser**. The hyphen (-) indicates using the same arguments passed through the pipe.

Options

-	Use the standard input of the command
-a_user_	Assign _user_ as user name
-b	Return the input if an error prevents successful completion of the command
-c	Copy the actual file directly (default)
-C	Copy _file_ to a spooling directory route to the ultimate destination
-g_p_	Set job priority to _p_
-j	Display job identifier
-n	Don't notify user upon completion
-p	Use the standard input of the command (same as -)
-r	Queue _file(s)_, but don't transfer them
-s_file_	Show status in _file_ (full pathname)
-x_n_	Set debugging level _n_
-z	Notify user on successful completion
_p_	Job priority (number or letter); lower number or letter indicates higher priority
_n_	Debug level: 0-9; 0 for least information, 9 for most

Note Once **uux** has executed the command on the other system, you will receive a status message. An exit code of zero (0) indicates successful completion.

See Also UNIX-to-UNIX copy (**uucp**)
UNIX-to-UNIX status (**uustat**)

UNIX-to-UNIX Log

```
$ uulog [-fsystem] [-n] [-ssystem] [-x] [system]
```

Use **uulog** to keep a log of **uucp** file transfers to and from *system*.

Application   To display all **uucp** activity on system **mars**, enter **uulog mars**. To display only the last 20 lines, enter **uulog -20 mars**.

Options

-f*system*	Generate **tail -f** of the file transfer for *system*
-*n*	Generate **tail** of the last *n* lines of the log
-s*system*	Display information about progress of the job running on *system*
-x	Find *system* in the **uuxqt** log file

Note   The log will tell you which jobs were completed successfully and which were not. It will also provide brief reasons for failures.

See Also   Display closing lines (**tail**, Chapter 3)
UNIX-to-UNIX copy (**uucp**)

UNIX-to-UNIX Status

```
$ uustat [-acmnpq] [-jn] [-kid] [-rn] [-dn] [-tsystem]
[-ssystem] [-Sflags] [-uuser]
```

Use **uustat** to display the status of **uucp** activity. By default, **uustat** shows only those jobs initiated by the same user who issues the **uustat** command.

Application   To display status for your own jobs, enter **uustat**. To kill one of the jobs displayed (say, job number 0384), enter **uustat -k 0384**.

To display status for jobs initiated by user **jason**, enter **uustat -u jason**. To display status for jobs associated with system **thor**, enter **uustat -s thor**.

Options

-a	Display status for **all** jobs, not just your own
-c	Display average time for all queues
-d*n*	Calculate in *n* minute intervals (default 60)
-j*n*	Display the total number of jobs shown
-k*id*	Kill job identifier *id*

-m	Show which systems can be accessed
-n	Show standard error, not standard output
-p	Run **ps -flp** on process ids in lock files
-q	Show job numbers, control files, and give longest and shortest times for files queued
-r*n*	Set time of modification for job *n* to the current time
-s*system*	Show status of **uucp** requests associated with *system*
-S*flags*	Display the status of each job:

c	Completed
i	Interrupted
q	Queued
r	Running

-t*system*	Show rate of transfer or queue time for *system*
-u*user*	Show status of **uucp** requests initiated by *user*

Only options **-s** and **-u** can be used on the same command line.

Note   Each line of the display shows the job number; the date and time; direction (S for send, R for receive); the name of the system; the originator; the size of the file; and the name of the file queued.

See Also   Send and receive mail (**mailx**)
UNIX-to-UNIX execute (**uux**)
UNIX-to-UNIX copy (**uucp**)

UNIX-to-UNIX System Names

```
$ uuname [-cl]
```

Use **uuname** to display the names of systems that you can access with **cu**, **mailx**, or **uucp**.

Application   To display all names that you can access, enter **uuname**. To restrict the names to those systems accessible by **cu**, enter **uuname -c**.

To display your own system name, enter **uuname -l**.

Options

-c	Display only names of systems available to **cu**
-l	Display the name of the local system

Note If you attempt to copy a file to a system not displayed by **uuname**, **uucp** will fail.

See Also Call up another system (**cu**)
Send and receive mail (**mailx**)
UNIX-to-UNIX copy (**uucp**)

Write to Another User

```
$ write user [terminal]
```

Use **write** to send a message to another user. The other user's terminal will beep, and the message will appear on the user's screen immediately.

Application To send a message to user **pat**, enter **write pat**, type your message, followed by **o** for "over," and terminate the message with **Ctrl D**. If **pat** works at more than one terminal, you can direct your message to one of them by entering **write pat /dev/tty09** (or something similar).

As long as **pat** isn't using one of the programs that blocks out screen messages, such as **vi** or **pr**, and hasn't explicitly blocked out messages with the **mesg** command, your message will appear. Then **pat** can respond with another **write** command to you, and so on. The convention is to follow the last message with **oo** for "over and out."

Notes The **write** command is most suitable for a single brief message. For an extended dialog with another user, **talk** is more appropriate. For a long, detailed message or set of instructions, **mailx** is the answer.

Note that **write** and **talk** provide instant communication, while messages sent via **mailx** may not arrive at their destinations for several hours, or even another day.

See Also Carry on a dialog (**talk**)
Send and receive mail (**mailx**)
Set terminal access (**mesg**)

8

System Administration

This chapter describes the commands used by system administrators to maintain a UNIX system. Only common commands used from day to day are included here. Some commands from earlier chapters are revisited here.

Note that the commands for maintaining printers are discussed in Chapter 6.

$ wall

Use **wall** (write-all) to write to all users on the system. The command is usually used to inform users of an imminent problem.

Application   To send a message that you type manually, enter **wall**, type the message, and terminate the message with **Ctrl D**. Here is an example:

> # **wall**
> **Third notice: the system is going down in five minutes.**
> **Ctrl D**
> # _

To send a message that you have already stored in a file called **notice**, enter **wall < notice**.

Note   Anyone can use the **wall** command, but the system administrator is usually the only one with a need to use it.

See Also   Write to another user (**write**)

Change Date and Time

```
$ date [-a][-]sss.fff] [-u] [MMdd]hhmm[yy]
```

Chapter 2 describes the use of **date** to display the date and time. In this chapter, you will learn how to use **date** to set the date and time.

Application To adjust the current time ahead three seconds, enter **date -a3.000**. To change the date to April 6, enter **date 0406**.

Options -a[-]sss.fff

Adjust the time by *sss.fff* or *-sss.fff* (in seconds and fractions of a second)

-u

Display the date and time in Greenwich Mean Time (GMT)

[*MMdd*]*hhmm*[*yy*]

Change the date and time as indicated (using month, day, hour, minute, year as required)

Note You can adjust the time by a small amount using the **-a** option. You can also change the date and time by any amount.

See Also Display date and time (**date**)

Change File-Access Permissions

```
$ chmod [-R] modes file(s)
```

Change file-access permissions (also called modes) for a given file, or group of files. The files can be either ordinary files or directories.

You can enter the *modes* argument in either symbolic form or in numeric form. In this chapter, we'll discuss only the numeric form. The symbolic form is covered in Chapter 3.

Application Chapter 3 covers the use of symbols to represent permissions. You can also use the following numeric codes:

400	owner read	040	group read
004	others read	200	owner write
020	group write	002	others write
100	owner execute	010	group execute
001	others execute		

By totaling the codes for the permissions granted, you can obtain a total in octal representation. The lowest total possible is 000 (access completely denied to everyone); the highest is 777 (access granted to everyone). The lowest **practical** total is 400 (owner read permission granted, all others denied).

As an example, suppose you want to grant the following permissions: rwxr-xr--. Using the table of values shown above, the total is 400 + 200 + 100 + 040 + 010 + 004 = 754. To grant these permissions for file **info**, enter **chmod 754 info**.

Here's another example: grant permissions rw-r----- for file **intro**. Total the numeric values: 400 + 200 + 040 = 640. Enter **chmod 640 intro**.

As a third example, grant permissions r--r--r-- for file **secret** (that is, make the file read-only). The total is 444 (400 + 040 + 004), so enter **chmod 444 secret**.

Option   -R   Descend recursively through directories

Note   Execute permission for a file enables you to run a program you have written.

See Also   Display files in a directory (**ls**, Chapter 3)
                  Change file ownership (**chown**)
                  Change file-access permissions (**chmod**, Chapter 3)
                  Change group (**chgrp**)

Change Group

```
$ chgrp [-hR] group file(s)
```

Use **chgrp** to change the group id of a file, or a set of files. The file (or files) can be a directory (or directories). Optionally, you can change the group id of subdirectories and files under a directory.

Application   To change the group for file **report** to **eng** (with id 50), enter **chgrp eng report** (or **chgrp 50 report**).

                  To change the group for directory **/u1/test/plans**, along with all its subdirectories and files, enter **chgrp -R eng /u1/test/plans** (or **chgrp -R 50 /u1/test/plans**).

Options	-h	Change for a symbolic link instead of a file
	-R	Change recursively through subdirectories and files
	group	Either the name or the numeric id of the group

Note   You can change only to a group you are already authorized to belong to. Otherwise, you have to get the superuser to allow you to be a member of the new group.

See Also Change owner (**chown**)
Change file-access permissions (**chmod**)

Change Owner

```
$ chown [-hR] owner file(s)
```

Use **chown** to change the ownership of a file, or a set of files. The file (or files) can be a directory (or directories). Optionally, you can change the ownership of subdirectories and files under a directory.

Application To change the owner for file **report** to **rob** (with id 14), enter **chown rob report** (or **chown 14 report**).

To change directory **/u1/test/plans**, along with all its subdirectories and files, to the same owner, enter **chown -R eng /u1/test/plans** (or **chown -R 14 /u1/test/plans**).

Options	-h	Change for a symbolic link instead of a file
	-R	Change recursively through subdirectories and files
	owner	Either the name or the numeric id of the owner

Note   Ordinary users can change ownership only of their own files; the superuser can change the ownership of any file.

See Also Change group (**chgrp**)
Change file-access permissions (**chmod**)

Change Password

```
$ passwd [-dfl] [-n min] [-x max] [-w warn] user
```

Chapter 2 described how to use **passwd** to change your own password. This chapter shows how to use **passwd** as superuser to change or delete any password on the system.

Application   To delete the password assigned to user **len**, enter
passwd -d len. To force the same password to expire,
enter **passwd -f len**.

Options   -d   Delete the password belonging to the user
                     named
           -f   Force the user's password to expire
           -l   Lock the user's password, preventing it from
                     being changed by the user
           -n *min*   Make *min* the minimum number of days
                     between password changes
           -a   Display password attributes for all users
           -w *notice* Set the number of days before expiration of
                     the password to notify the user named
           -x *max*   Set the maximum number of days the user
                     can use the password

Note   It is the system administrator's responsibility to enforce
       the use of passwords and to set up password aging. The
       most secure UNIX system is one on which all users have
       passwords and change them at regular intervals. As a
       system administrator, you will have to find the right
       balance between security and convenience.

See Also   Change password (**passwd**, Chapter 2)

Change System Name

```
$ uname [-S system]
```

Chapter 2 describes the use of **uname** to display information about your
system. This chapter describes the use of **uname** to change the name of
your system.

Application   To change the name of your system to **neptune**, enter
uname -S neptune.

Option   -S *system*   Change name of your system to *system*

Note   You may not be able to use this option on all UNIX
       systems.

See Also   Display system name (**uname**, Chapter 2)

Change Terminal Settings

```
$ stty [-a] [-g] [mode(s)]
```

Chapter 2 covered the use of **stty** for displaying terminal settings already in effect and making simple changes. This chapter describes comprehensively the use of **stty** to change operational settings for your terminal.

Application   To display all of your terminal's operational settings, enter **stty -a**. To display information that can be used as an argument for a subsequent **stty** command, enter **stty -g**.

To notify the system of a change in the operation of your terminal, you can enter one or more of a set of more than 70 modes. For example, to indicate a change in character size to 8 bits, you can enter **stty cs8**.

Options   -a   All: display all terminal settings
-g   Display settings in a format suitable for use as an argument for the **stty** command

Terminal modes:
The following modes are independent of the direction of data flow:

0 (zero)	Hang up
async	Set asynchronous mode, plus **rcibrg**, **rsetcoff**, **tsetcoff**, and **xcibrg**
[-]**raw**	[Disable/]enable raw input and output
[-]**tabs**	[Convert tabs to spaces/]preserve tabs
[-]**lcase**	[Do not] change case (same as [-]**xcase**, [-]**iuclc**, and [-]**olcuc**)
[-]**LCASE**	[Do not] change case (same as [-]**lcase**)
[-]**nl**	[Do not] convert input carriage returns to newlines or output newlines to carriage returns
[-]**parenb**	[Disable/]enable parity detection
[-]**parodd**	[Disable/]enable odd parity
[-]**parity**	[Disable/]enable **parenb**; set **cs** to [8/]7
[-]**evenp**	[Disable/]enable **parenb**; set **cs** to [8/]7
[-]**oddp**	[Disable/]enable **parenb**; set **cs** to [7/]8
[-]**cread**	[Disable/]enable receiver
[-]**clocal**	[Disable/]enable modem control

[-]cstopb	Use [one/]two stop bits
[-]hup	[Do not] hang up on the last close
[-]hupcl	[Do not] hang up on the last close (same as [-]hup)
[-]loblk	[Do not] block ouput from a noncurrent layer

Terminal input modes:

[-]brkint	[Do not] cause the break key to send an interrupt signal to the current process
[-]icrnl	[Do not] convert carriage returns to newlines
[-]ignbrk	[Do not] ignore break
[-]igncr	[Do not] ignore carriage returns
[-]ignpar	[Do not] ignore parity errors
[-]inlcr	[Do not] convert newlines to carriage returns
[-]inpck	[Do not] enable parity checking
[-]istrip	[Do not] strip characters of eighth bit
[-]iuclc	[Do not] convert uppercase to lowercase
[-]ixany	Use [XON/]any character to restart output
[-]ixoff	[Disable/]enable XON/XOFF input control
[-]ixon	[Disable/]enable XON/XOFF output control
[-]parmrk	[Do not] mark parity errors

Terminal output mode:

bs$n$	Output delay after backspace is n (0 or 1)
cr$n$	Output delay after carriage return is n (0-3)
ff$n$	Output delay after formfeed is n (0 or 1)
nl$n$	Output delay after newline is n (0 or 1)
[-]ocrnl	[Do not] convert carriage returns to newlines
[-]ofdel	Set fill characters to [null/]**Del**
[-]ofill	Use [timing/]fill characters for delay
[-]cdxon	Turn [off/]on output flow control for CD
[-]olcuc	[Do not] convert lowercase to uppercase
[-]onlcr	[Do not] convert newlines to carriage returns
[-]onlret	[Do not] insert a carriage return after each newline
[-]onocr	[Do not] output a carriage return at column zero

[-]opost	[Do not] post-process output
tab*n*	Set output delay after *n* horizontal tabs (0-3)
vt*n*	Set output delay after *n* vertical tabs (0 or 1)

Local operations control modes:

[-]echo	[Do not] echo keyboard input
[-]echok	[Do not] echo newline after the kill character
[-]echol	[Do not] echo newlines
[-]icanon	[Disable/]enable erase and kill characters
[-]isig	[Disable/]enable checking for interrupt and quit
[-]lfkc	[Do not] echo newline after the kill character
[-]noflsh	[Do not] flush buffers after interrupt and quit
[-]stappl	Use [line/]application mode on a synchronous line
[-]lstflsh	[Disable/]enable flush on a synchronous line
[-]strap	[Enable/]disable truncation of long lines on a synchronous line
[-]xcase	[Do not] change case for local input

Control characters:

ctab *c*	Make *c* the control tab character
ek	Make # the erase character and @ the kill character
eof *c*	Make *c* the end-of-file (EOF) character (default **Ctrl D**)
eol *c*	Make *c* the end-of-line (EOL) character (default null)
erase *c*	Make *c* the erase character (default #)
intr *c*	Make *c* the interrupt signal (default RUBOUT)
kill *c*	Make *c* the kill character, which erases an input line (default @)
quit *c*	Make *c* the quit signal (default **Ctrl **)

Note   If you are accustomed to DOS, you have no doubt noticed that there are far more modes available with **stty** than you ever even imagined on a DOS system. The gobbledygook in this section is not intended for novices.

See Also   Display terminal settings (**stty**, Chapter 2)

Control Terminal

```
$ tput [-Ttype] [cap[param]]
```

Use **tput** to display the operational capabilities of your terminal, control the operation of your terminal, or initialize your terminal. The command relies on the contents of the terminal information file for your terminal (**/usr/lib/terminfo/*/***).

Application To clear your terminal's screen and move the cursor to the home position, enter **tput clear**. To move the cursor to line 12, column 40 (the middle of the screen), enter **tput cup 12 40**. To display your terminal's long name, enter **tput longname**.

Options -T*type*   Specify terminal *type* (default **$TERM**)
  cap   A terminal capability specified for your terminal in **/usr/lib/terminfo/*/*** (partial list shown below)
  param Parameters required for *cap*

Terminal capabilities:
The following capabilities relate to terminal features.

lines Number of screen lines
cols   Number of screen columns

The following capabilities relate to cursor movement.

home   Move the cursor to home position
clear   Clear the screen and move the cursor to home position
cup *r c* Move cursor to row *r*, column *c*
vpa *r*   Move cursor to row *r*
hpa *c*   Move cursor to column *c*
ht   Move cursor to the next tab
cbt   Move cursor to the previous tab
cr   Carriage return

The following capabilities relate to screen editing:

el   Clear to end of line
ed   Clear to end of screen
clear   Clear the screen and move the cursor to home
          position
smir   Begin insert mode
rmir   End insert mode
smdc   Begin delete mode
rmdc   End delete mode

The following capabilities relate to video attributes:

bold   Begin bold mode
dim   Begin dim mode
blink   Begin blink mode
smso   Begin standout mode
smul   Begin underscore mode
rev   Begin reverse video mode
prot   Begin protected mode
rmso   End standout mode
rmul   End underscore mode
sgr0   End all attributes

The following directives control your terminal:

as   Start alternate character set
ae   End alternate character set
init   Initialize your terminal
longname Display the long name of your terminal
reset   Reset your terminal
tc *def* Use another **terminfo** definition
vs   Start **vi**
ve   End **vi**

Note   The **tput** command is an excellent tool for controlling
          your terminal. Many of its uses involve programming,
          which is not covered in this book.

See Also Change terminal settings (**stty**)
            Display terminal settings (**stty**, Chapter 2)
            Set terminal tabs (**tabs**)

Copy and Convert a File

```
$ dd    [option(s)]
```

Use **dd** to copy files from one location to another or from one device to another. If the two locations or devices contain incompatible data, **dd** can also convert from one to the other.

The conversions that **dd** can handle include the following: different byte order in words, different block sizes, different case, and different character coding (such as ASCII and EBCDIC).

Application To copy a file called **start** to another called **finish** and convert lowercase letters to uppercase, enter **dd conv=ucase if=start of=finish** (or **dd conv=ucase < start > finish**).

A number of options enable you to handle differences between media and machines. For example, to convert EBCDIC data stored on tape from an IBM mainframe to a UNIX file called **data.ibm**, you could enter a command line like the following:

$ dd if=/dev/rmt/mt1 of=data.ibm ibs=800 cbs=80 conv=ascii,lcase

The magnetic tape is on the tape drive represented by device file **/dev/rmt/mt1**. The target file is **data.ibm** in the current directory. The input is 80-character records with 10 records per block (800-character blocks). Finally, EBCDIC character codes will be converted to ASCII and uppercase letters will be converted to lowercase.

Options

bs=n	Set the block size to n bytes for input and output	
cbs=n	Conversion buffer size, or length of logical records, is n bytes	
conv=	Convert (use commas to separate more than one):	
	ascii	EBCDIC to ASCII
	block	Variable-length to fixed-length records
	ebcdic	ASCII to EBCDIC
	ibm	ASCII to a variant of EBCDIC
	lcase	Uppercase to lowercase

	noerror	Keep converting even if an error occurs
	swab	Swap bytes within words
	sync	Pad each input record to fit **ibs** value
	ucase	Lowercase to uppercase
	unblock	Fixed-length to variable-length records
count=*n*		Copy no more than *n* input records
files=*n*		Copy no more than *n* input files to tape
ibs=*n*		Input block size is *n* bytes (default 512)
iseek=*n*		Seek *n* input blocks before starting to copy
obs=*n*		Output block size is *n* bytes (default 512)
of=*file*		Send output to *file* (default standard output)
oseek=*n*		Seek *n* output blocks before starting to copy
seek=*n*		Same as **oseek**
skip=*n*		Skip *n* input blocks
n		Number of bytes (with an optional block size appended):
	*n***b**	512-byte blocks
	*n***k**	1024-byte blocks
	*n***w**	2-byte blocks (words)

Note   The conversion options of **dd** make it more suitable than other copy commands for copying to and from non-UNIX systems.

See Also   Copy input/output (**cpio**)
Translate characters (**tr**)

Copy Input/Output

```
$ cpio -i[6bBcdfkmrsStuvV] [-C n] [-E file] [-H hdr]
[-I file] [-O file] [-M message] [-R id] [patterns]
$ cpio -o[aABcLvV] [-C size] [-H hdr] [-O file] [-M message]
$ cpio -p[adlmruvV] [-R id] directory
```

Use **cpio** to copy files between your working system and backup storage; you can also use **cpio** to copy directories from one place to another. The command operates in three different modes, as indicated by the three *keys* just shown:

•   Copy in (**cpio -i**): copy files from storage to the system

- Copy out (**cpio -o**): copy files from the system to storage
- Pass (**cpio -p**): copy from one directory to another

Application   The **cpio** command nearly always receives its input from another command through a pipe. (If a file contains a list of filenames, you can also redirect input from that file.) We'll cover each of the three modes of **cpio** in reverse order.

To copy all the files in the current directory to another directory under the same parent, called **storage**, enter **find . -print | cpio -pv ../storage**. The verbose option (**-v**) causes the name of each file copied to be displayed.

To back all files in the current directory to tape, use an entry something like this: **find . -print | cpio -oBv > /dev/rmt/2**. This command line includes options for blocking (**-B**) and verbose output (**-v**).

To recover the files already backed up to tape, use an entry something like this: **cpio -iBv < /dev/rmt/2**.

Options

-6	Recover files in UNIX Version 6 format
-a	Reset access times of files to their original times
-A	Use with **-O** to append to the output
-b	Reverse order of bytes within a word
-B	Use 5,120-byte blocks for tape archive
-c	Generate ASCII header information
-C *n*	Use *n*-byte records for tape archive
-d	Create target directories as required
-E *file*	Read list of filenames to extract from *file*
-f	Copy only files that do **not** match the *patterns*
-H *hdr*	Read or write headers in one of four formats:

	crc	ASCII with expanded device numbers and checksums
	ustar	IEEE/P1003 Data Interchange Standard
	tar	Unix **tar** format
	odc	ASCII with small device numbers

-I *file*	Read *file* as an input archive
-k	Skip unreadable file headers if possible
-l	Link, rather than copy, the files if possible

-L	Follow symbolic links
-m	Retain original modification times of files
-M *message*	Use with **-I** or **-O** to prompt for a tape or disk switch (**%d** means sequence number)
-O *file*	Send output to *file*
-r	Rename files interactively
-R *id*	Assign a new owner and group (only the superuser can do this)
-s	Swap bytes within each half word
-S	Swap half words within each word
-t	Show table of contents only; do not copy
-u	Copy unconditionally, without regard to timestamps
-v	Verbose: Display names of files being copied
-V	Tiny verbose: Display a dot for each file copied

Notes　　The **cpio** command accepts input from any command that provides a list of filenames. The most commonly used commands are **cat**, **find**, and **ls**.

To send **cpio** through the current directory and all its subdirectories, you can use **find** with its **-depth** option, as shown in this example: **find . -depth -print | cpio -oBv > /dev/rmt/1**.

See Also　　Concatenate files (**cat**, Chapter 3)
Copy files (**cp**, Chapter 3)
Display files in a directory (**ls**, Chapter 4)
Find files (**find**, Chapter 4)
Tape archive (**tar**)

Create Environment

```
$ env [-] [var=value, ...] [command line]
```

The environment refers collectively to the settings for a variety of shell variables, such as your login directory, login name, mail box, terminal type, command path, and default shell. Any time you change even one of these variables, you change your environment.

Use **env** to assign new values to shell variables (thereby creating a new environment), pass the new environment to a UNIX command (including **env** itself), and execute the command. You have the option of either passing the entire new environment to the target command or restricting the new environment for the target command to those shell variables explicitly changed on the **env** command line.

If you omit the variable assignments and command line, you can display the current environment.

Application   To display the current environment, enter **env** alone without any options.

To change your home directory to **/u1/mktg/ben** and your default shell to the C shell, then execute **who** in the new environment, enter **env HOME=/u1/mktg/ben SHELL=/bin/csh who**.

Options   -   Use only the values changed on this command line

var=value   Assign a new value to one shell variable

command line   Any UNIX command line

Note   The **env** allows you to test a command line under different environments before making the changes permanent.

Create File Creation Mask

```
$ umask [ugo]
```

Use **umask** to create a file creation mask, which determines the default permissions of all files stored on the system. The **umask** permission option *ugo* works the opposite of the same option for **chmod**. With **umask**, *ugo* **denies** permissions for user, group, and others; with **chmod**, *ugo* **grants** permissions.

Application   To display the current value of the file creation mask, enter **umask** without an argument. The default value is 022, which means permissions of 755 for new files created (if system default is 777, 022 + 755 = 777).

To set a file creation mask of 034, enter **umask 034**.

Option   *ugo*   Octal permission codes for user (*u*), group (*g*), and others (*o*).

Each code is a sum of codes to deny permission for read (4), write (2), and execute (1).

Note   Rather than execute **umask** on a command line, you usually place it in the system's initialization file (**/etc/profile**), where it will be executed automatically during system start-up.

See Also Change file-access permissions (**chmod**)

Display Disk Usage

```
$ du [-ars] [file(s)] [dir(s)]
```

Use **du** to display the amount of disk space (in blocks) used by each directory (and optionally by each file in each directory).

Application To display the amount of disk space occupied by each subdirectory in the current directory, enter **du**.

Options   -a   Allow filenames also
              -r   Display a message for any directory that is unreadable
              -s   Summary only

Note   You can use **du** to discover space hogs on your system. (*Space hogs* are users who use an excessive amount of disk space, not porcine aliens.)

See Also Display free blocks (**df**)

```
/usr/nelson> du -a
1       ./.profile
1       ./.elm/elmrc
1       ./.elm/signature
3       ./.elm
3       ./.sh_history
1       ./calendar
1       ./test/algebra
1       ./test/info
1       ./test/jagged
1       ./test/sample
5       ./test
1       ./text
1       ./entry/sample
1       ./entry/sales
1       ./entry/market
1       ./entry/salesmkt
1       ./entry/mktsales
6       ./entry
1       ./new/test
1       ./new/name
1       ./new/phone
1       ./new/list
1       ./new/fruits
```

An example of the du command

Display Free Space

```
$ df [-F type] [-begklntV] [-o option(s)] [file_system(s)]
```

Use **df** to display information about the amount of free space on a file system, or a set of file systems. Depending on which options you choose, you can display the total amount of space, the amount used, and the amount free in blocks, i-nodes, or kilobytes. You can also display the amounts in percentages and the name of the device on which each file system is mounted.

Application   To check free space for each directory of the your file system, enter **df**. The resulting display will show the name of each major directory, its device name, and the number of blocks and i-nodes available. The number of i-nodes available is the number of additional files you can create.

To include total space, enter **df -t**. The resulting display will be similar to that for **df**. But it will also include for each major directory the total number of blocks and i-nodes.

Options
-b	Display only the number of kilobytes free
-e	Display only the number of files free
-F *type*	For unmounted file systems, indicate *type*
-g	For unmounted file systems, display the entire **statvfs** structure
-k	Display allocation in kilobytes
-l	For mounted file systems, report on local file systems only
-n	Display *type* of file system only
-o *option(s)*	Specify *option(s)* specific to the file system *type*
file_system(s)	The name of the device on which a file system is mounted; the name of the directory where the file system is mounted; the name of a Network File System (NFS) or Remote File Sharing (RFS) resource.

Note   If users in a file system are running out of disk space, you can use **df** to locate areas where you can cut down. If you find directories or files that are taking up excessive space, you can move or delete them.

See Also   Display disk usage (**du**)

```
/usr/nelson> df
Filesystem          kbytes     used   avail capacity  Mounted on
/dev/sd0a            15671    10452    3652    74%    /
/dev/sd0b            94743    83367    1902    98%    /usr
/dev/sd1a           161055    59114   85836    41%    /var/spool/mail
/dev/sd1b           131359     2094  116130     2%    /usr/tmp
/dev/sd1c           104575    79670   14448    85%    /usr/acc
/dev/sd1d           236623   140349   72612    66%    /usr/local
/dev/sd1e           893574   177189  627028    22%    /home
/dev/sd2a           236623   201013   11948    94%    /usr1
/dev/sd2b           236623   180200   32761    85%    /usr2
/dev/sd2c           236623   182388   30573    86%    /usr3
/dev/sd2d           246099   182773   38717    83%    /usr4
```

An example of the df command

Display Ids

```
$ id [-a]
```

Use **id** to display your user id (and name) and group id (and name).

Application To display your user and group ids, enter **id**. To display all groups you belong to, enter **id -a**. If you belong to more than one group, all the ids and names will be displayed.

Option **-a** Display all groups

See Also Display login name (**logname**)
Display users (**who**)

```
/usr/nelson> id
uid=2772(nelson) gid=50(users0) groups=50(users0)
```

An example of the id command

Display Login Name

```
$ logname
```

Use **logname** to display your login name (the value of shell variable $LOGNAME).

Application To display your login name, enter **logname**.

See Also Log into system (**login**, Chapter 2)
Create environment (**env**)

Display Name of Terminal

```
$ tty [-ls]
```

Use **tty** to display the pathname for your terminal.

Application   To display the name of your terminal, enter **tty**.

Options   **-l**   The terminal is on a synchronous, instead of an
                       asynchronous, line
              -s   Silent mode: Suppress output

Note   You can use **tty** to identify a terminal's pathname before
               sending output to it.

Display Time for a Command

```
$ time command
$ timex [-ops] command
```

Use **time** and **timex** to display the amount of time a UNIX command
takes to execute (elapsed time, user time, and system time). With **timex**,
you can also display the number of blocks read and written, system
activity, and accounting information.

Application   To display the amount of time it takes to print file report
                  in two columns, enter **timex pr -2 report | lp**.

                  To display the amount of time it takes to check the
                  spelling of text file **behemoth**, enter **timex spell
                  behemoth**.

Options   **-o**   Display number of blocks read and written and
                            number of characters transferred
              -p [*opt*] Show process activity for *command* and all its
                            children, using the following suboptions:
                  -f   Show *exec/fork* flag and exit status
                  -h   Show CPU time divided by elapsed time
                  -k   Show kcore time in minutes
                  -m   Show mean core size
                  -r   Show user time divided by (system time +
                           user time)

149

-t	Show CPU and system times, plus the number of blocks read and written
-s	Use **sar** to display system activity during the execution of *command*

Note The **timex** command, which has superseded the older **time** command, gives you a handy tool for gauging the time consumed by specific processes and users.

```
/usr/nelson/text> time spell sample

real    0m1.56s
user    0m0.08s
sys     0m0.66s
```

An example of the time command

Display User Names

```
$ who [am i] [-abdHlpqrstTu] [-n x] [file]
```

Use **who** to display the names of all users currently logged onto your UNIX system; optionally, display your login name; optionally, display a variety of other information.

Application To display who is logged onto your system, enter the **who** command without an argument (or with the default **-s** option).

To display the same information, along with idle time for each terminal, enter **who -u**.

Options

am i	Display your own login name.
-a	Display all information about logged in users (equivalent to **-bdHlpqrstTu**)
-b	Show the last date and time the system was booted
-d	Display processes that have expired, but have not been restarted by **init**
-H	Display column headings above the information shown
-l	Display all lines that are available for login
-n *x*	Display *x* users per line

-p   Display any processes started by **init** that are currently active

-q   Quick **who**: Names and user count only

-r   Display the current run-level of **init**

-s   Display current user's login name, terminal line, and time logged in (default option)

-t   Display the last time the system administrator used the **date** command to change the system clock

-T   Same as **-s**, plus the current state of each terminal:

        +   Any user can write to the terminal

        -     Only the system administrator can write to the terminal

        ?   Something is wrong with the terminal line

-u   Same as **-s**, plus the time since the last activity on the terminal line

file   Ordinarily, **who** gathers its information from the **/var/adm/utmp** file. If you want to name another file in its place here, you can (provided that it's in the same format).

Notes   You can use **who** to find out who is logged in, who is currently working, the last time a user was active, the last time the system was booted, how many terminal lines are available, or the total number of users logged in.

You can use any of this information in a shell script to make programming decisions.

See Also   Change date and time (**date**)
Display date and time (**date**, Chapter 2)
Log into system (**login**, Chapter 2)
Set terminal access (**mesg**, Chapter 2)

Find Information About Users

```
$ finger [-bfhilmpqsw] [user(s)]
$ finger [-l] "user@system"
```

Use **finger** to display information about one user or about all users on the system. The default is all users and the following information: user name, full name, terminal, terminal access, current idle time, time of login, office, phone number.

If you include at least one user name, **finger** will also display each user's home directory, login shell, **.plan**, and **.project** file.

You can also display information on a user on another system on the same network as your system.

Application To display information on all users, enter **finger**. To display a long report on user **jesse**, enter **finger -l jesse**.

Options
-b	Long display, minus home directory and login shell
-f	Short display, minus header
-h	Long display, minus **.project** file
-i	Idle display: only user name, terminal, time of login, and idle lines
-l	Long display
-m	Match only user name
-p	Long display, minus **.plan** file
-q	Quick display: Only user name, terminal, and time of login
-s	Short display
-w	Short format, minus full user name

Note The **.project** file usually describes the user's current working project. The **.plan** file usually describes future working projects.

See Also Display user names (**who**, Chapter 2)
Change user names (**who**)

```
/usr/nelson/text> finger

ls -l
Login      Name              TTY Idle   When     Where
tomg       Thomas Garson     00         Mon 21:46 ARCNet-sm3
djp        Daren Parkinson   01         Mon 22:46 ARCNet-la1
srengst    Sameul Rengstorff 02         Mon 22:32 ARCNet-sm4
parks      Bill Parks        03         Mon 22:16 ARCNet-la1
gonzo      Gonzales Ortega   04         Mon 23:03 ARCNet-la2
bull       Charles Evans     05 5:08    Mon 17:58 137.240.210.325
barns      Allen Barns       06         Mon 23:07 ARCNet-sm1
alg        Allan Gordon      07    4    Mon 21:42 ARCNet-oc1
tiger      Gary Martin       08         Mon 17:00 ARCNet-sb1
arz        Arlen Ziff        09         Mon 23:04 ARCNet-la1
```

An example of the finger command

Run Scheduled Processes

```
$ crontab [-elr] [file]
```

Use **crontab** to create a file, also called **crontab**, which contains a list of control lines. Each line includes a time code and a command to be executed. A daemon called **cron** reads the **crontab** file and executes each command at the time(s) indicated.

Application   To enter information into the **crontab** file, enter **crontab**. You can now enter control lines followed by **Ctrl D** to terminate text entry.

Each line in the file contains six fields, separated by spaces or tabs. The fields and allowable values are as follows:

Minutes	0-59
Hours	0-23
Day of month	1-31
Month of year	1-12
Day of week	0-6
UNIX command	N/A

An asterisk (*) in one of the time fields indicates all of the times (for example, every hour, every day, every month, and so on).

Options   -e   Edit the **crontab** file, using the editor assigned to the EDITOR variable

-l   List the contents of the **crontab** file

-r   Remove the **crontab** file

Note   The system administrator for each system decides which users are allowed to execute the **crontab** command.

Set Process Priority

$ nice [-n] *command* [*option(s)*] [*arg(s)*]

Use **nice** to change the priority of a process when executing it. Ordinary users can only lower the priority; the superuser can lower it or raise it.

Application The default priority level of each process is 20. A higher number indicates a lower priority; a lower number indicates a higher priority. To lower by 10 the priority of the process generated by **troff behemoth | lp**, enter **nice troff behemoth | lp**.

Option -*n* Decrease the priority by *n* (1-19) (default 10)

Notes Use **nice** with big jobs that require a lot of processing to allow smaller jobs to complete rapidly. The command enables one user to be **nice** to other users on the system.

The superuser can raise the priority of a process by entering --*n* instead of -*n* as an option.

See Also Check process status (**ps**, Chapter 2)

Set Terminal Tabs

$ tabs [*tabs*] [+m[*n*]] [+T*type*]

By default, terminal tabs in a UNIX system are set to every eighth column (1, 9, 17, 25, and so on). If your terminal has hardware tab stops that the host can control, you can use **tabs** to set the tabs in a different configuration. This can be especially helpful for entering program code that has strict formatting requirements.

Application To set up tabs for FORTRAN program, enter **tabs -f**. To move the left margin out to column 11, enter **tabs +m** (or **tabs +m10**).

Options For the *tabs* option, you can choose preset tabs:

-8 Every eighth column (1, 9, 17, . . ., 73)
-a IBM S/370 assembler (1, 10, 16, 36, 72)
-a2 IBM S/370 assembler 2 (1, 10, 16, 40, 72)
-c Normal COBOL (1, 8, 12, 16, 20, 55)

-c2	Compact COBOL (1, 6, 10, 14, 49)
-c3	Expanded COBOL (1, 6, 10, 14, 18, 22, 26, 30, 34, 38, 42, 46, 50, 54, 58, 62, 67)
-f	FORTRAN (1, 7, 11, 15, 19, 23)
-p	PL/1 (1, 5, 9, 13, 17, 21, 25, 29, 33, 37, 41, 45, 49, 53, 57, 61)
-s	SNOBOL (1, 10, 55)
-u	UNIVAC 1100 assembler (1, 12, 20, 44)

For the *tabs* option, you can also choose evenly spaced tabs, unevenly spaced tabs, or tabs read from a file:

-n	Every *n*th column (0 for no tabs)
a,b, . . .	Tabs at columns *a*, *b*, and so on (40 maximum)
--file	Tabs indicated on the first line of *file*

You can also choose one of two additional options:

+m[*n*]	Add *n* to the left margin (default 10)
-T[*type*]	Use default tabs for terminal *type*, which must be defined in **/usr/lib/terminfo/*/*** (default $TERM).

Note   You can select one set of tabs for your screen display using **tabs** and another set of tabs for printed output using **pr**.

See Also   Change terminal settings (**stty**)
Control terminal (**tput**)
Prepare files for printing (**pr**, Chapter 6)

Tape Archive

```
$ tar key[option(s)] device file(s)
```

Use **tar** to archive files on the file system to tape or disk. The tape can be either in a cartridge or on a 9-track reel. During file backup, you can either replace files already stored or append new files to an existing archive.

You can also use **tar** to recover files from backup, with options for selecting either the newest modification of a file or an earlier version.

In the descriptions that follow in this section, the word "tape" indicates the archive medium, whether it be tape, disk, or diskette.

Tape Archive

Application To back up to a high-density tape drive a set of files in the current directory called **report.jan, report.feb, report.mar,** and so on, enter **tar -cvf /dev/mt/0h report.*.** To restore these same files to the current directory at a later date, enter **tar -xvf /dev/mt/0h report.*.**

To back up the contents of the current directory to the same tape drive, enter **tar -cvf /dev/mt/0h *.** To restore these same files, enter **tar -xvf /dev/mt/0h.** (If you use ***** as shown, **tar** will copy all files except those that begin with a period (.), such as **.login**. To include these files, replace ***** with **.** in the **tar** command line.)

Function keys:

-c   Create a new tape and write *file(s)* (-r implied)
-r   Write *file(s)* to the end of the tape archive, leaving existing files intact
-t   Display a table of contents of the tape archive
-u   Update the archive tape by appending *file(s)* if they are not already on tape or if they have since been modified
-x   Extract *file(s)* from tape (all files if *file(s)* omitted

Options The following options, which you append to the function key, modify the operation of the key:

-b*f*   Set blocking facter to *f* (1-64; default 1)
-f*dev*   Use *dev* as archive device; if *dev* is -, use standard output (or input for recovery) (default **/dev/mt/***nd*)
-l   Display a message if **tar** cannot find all links on create, write, or update
-L   Follow symbolic links
-m   Update time of last modification to current time
-o   Change user and group id to your own on extraction
-v   Verbose mode: display names of files copied
-w   Wait for confirmation (**y**) for each individual file

nd	Tape drive (*n*) (0-7; default 0) and tape density: **h** High density (6250 bpi) **m** Medium density (1600 bpi) (default) **l** Low density (800 bpi)
dev	The target device for archive, which can be one of the following:

/dev/dsk/*n*	Hard disk *n* (block device)
/dev/rdsk/*n*	Raw hard disk *n* (character device)
/dev/mt/*nd*	Magnetic tape *n* (**h**, **m**, or **l** density)
/dev/rmt/*nd*	Raw magnetic tape *n* (**h**, **m**, or **l** density)
/dev/ctape	Cartridge tape
/dev/diskette	Diskette

Note   It is best to write to or read tape in single-user mode because the process will have priority over almost every other process on the system. If you are using a streaming tape cartridge, allow retensioning to complete before using **tar**.

See Also   Copy and convert a file (**dd**)
Copy input/output (**cpio**)

Update File-Access Times

```
$ touch [-acm] [MMddhhmm[yy]] file(s)
```

Use **touch** to update files' timestamps. You can update access time only, modification only, or both. If you name a file that doesn't already exist, **touch** can create it.

Application   To update the timestamps for file **past** to the current date and time, enter **touch past**. To update the times to 3:48 p.m. on May 24, 1993, enter **touch 0524154893 past**.

To create a new file called **zero**, enter **touch zero**. The file will show the current date and time, and will show a size of 0.

Options

-a	Update access time only
-c	If a file does not already exist, do not create it
-m	Update modification time only
MMddhhmm[yy]	New date and time to be used instead of the current date and time:

	MM	Month (1-12)
	dd	Day of the month (1-31)
	hh	Hour (00-23)
	mm	Minute (00-59)
	yy	Year (00-99)

Notes

The purpose of updating timestamps for a file could be to prevent the file from being deleted. Some processes automatically remove all files beyond a certain age. With **touch**, you can update the timestamps and spare the file from deletion.

The purpose of creating an empty file could be to satisfy a shell script that requires a file for locking or time-comparison.

See Also

Display date and time (**date**, Chapter 2)
Display files in a directory (**ls**, Chapter 3)

The UNIX Locator

Appendix A provides the names of the major directories and tells you where to find key files and directories in a UNIX system.

Major Directories

The following directories are found on nearly all UNIX systems. Most subdirectories and files are located in these major directories.

Administrative directory	**/etc/***
System executable program (binary) directory	**/bin/***
Device directory	**/dev/***
Temporary file directory	**/tmp/***
User directory	**/usr/***
Application executable program (binary) directory	**/usr/bin/***
Variable directory	**/var/***

Commonly Used Files and Directories

If you need to find an important file or directory, you can look for its name in this section. Just look up the function of the file or directory on the left; its name will be shown across from it on the right.

Accounting
      Information on users   **/var/adm/utmp/var/adm/wtmp**
      System activity reporting (**sar**)   **/usr/lib/sa**
          Log files for **sar**   **/var/adm/sa**
      Utilities   **/usr/lib/acct**

Bourne shell   **/bin/sh**

C shell	**/bin/csh**
cron directory	**/usr/sbin/cron.d**
Accounting information	**/usr/sbin/cron.d/log**
Control information	**/usr/spool/cron/crontabs**
Timed processes	**/usr/lib/crontab**
Users allowed	**/usr/sbin/cron.d/allow**
Users denied	**/usr/sbin/cron.d/deny**
Cross reference file	**/etc/magic**
Date file	**/usr/lib/calprog**
Device directory	**/dev/***
Hard drive subdirectory (block)	**/dev/dsk/***
Hard drive subdirectory (raw)	**/dev/rdsk/***
Magnetic tape subdirectory (block)	**/dev/mt/***
Magnetic tape subdirectory (raw)	**/dev/rmt/***
Terminals	**/dev/**tty*nn*
Virtual console	**/dev/syscon**
ex and **vi**	
Error messages	**/usr/lib/ex?.?strings**
Initialization file	**$HOME/.exrc**
Preserve command	**/usr/lib/ex?.?preserve**
Preserved files	**/var/preserve/***user*
Recover command	**/usr/lib/ex?.?recover**
Temporary storage files	**/tmp/Rx***nnnnn*
Temporary work buffer	**/tmp/EX***nnnnn*
Terminal information	**/usr/share/lib/terminfo/?/***
Failed login log	**/var/adm/loginlog**
File systems	
Currently mounted file systems	**/etc/mnttab**
Default parameters for file systems	**/etc/vfstab**
Disk partitions with file systems	**/dev/dsk/***
File systems to be mounted	**/etc/checklist**
Group file	**/etc/group**
Kernel file	**/unix**
Korn shell	**/bin/ksh**
Last login times	**/var/adm/lastlog**

Mail system
    Help messages   **/usr/lib/mailx/mailx.help***
    Initialization file   **/usr/lib/mailx/mailx.rc**
    Mailbox for *user*   **/usr/mail/*user***
    Temporary files   **/tmp/R[emqsw]***

Memory
    System memory   **/dev/mem**
    Virtual memory for kernel   **/dev/kmem**

Message of the day file   **/etc/motd**

more command help file   **/usr/lib/more.help**

Mount table file   **/etc/mounttab**

news command
    Last time of perusal   **$HOME/.news_time**
    News items   **/usr/news/***

Passwords
    Password file   **/etc/passwd**
    Secure password information   **/etc/shadow**

Printers
    Print request file   **/usr/spool/lp/request**
    Command directory   **/usr/lib/***
    Printer interface programs   **/usr/spool/lp/interface/***
    Spooling system directory   **/usr/spool/lp/***

sort command temporary file   **/usr/tmp/stm***

Spelling directory   **/usr/lib/spell**

su command log   **/var/adm/sulog**

System
    Initialization file   **/etc/rc**
    Initialization table   **/etc/inittab**
    Login file (read by **csh**)   **/etc/login**
    Profile file (read by **sh**/**ksh**)   **/etc/profile**
    Kernel file   **/unix**

tar command temporary file   **/tmp/tar***

Temporary files   **/tmp/***
                                                       /usr/tmp/*

Terminals
Default information	/etc/gettydefs
Escape sequences for margins and tabs	/usr/lib/tabset/*
Information (previous releases)	/etc/termcap
Information (standard)	/usr/share/lib/terminfo/?/*
Initialization	/etc/profile
Lines	/etc/inittab

Timed processes	/usr/lib/crontab

Users
Accounting information	/var/adm/utmp/var/adm/wtmp
Mailbox for *user*	/var/mail/*user*
User information file	/etc/passwd
User login file (read by **csh**)	$HOME/.login
User profile (read by **sh** and **ksh**)	$HOME/.profile
Who file	/etc/utmp

Virtual console	/dev/syscon

Who file	/etc/utmp

B

The Bourne Shell

Appendix B summarizes the command processor for the original UNIX system, which is known as the Bourne shell.

```
$ sh [option(s)] [argument(s)]
```

Options

	-a	Mark modified export variables
	-c *command*	Execute *command*; default is the first argument
	-e	Exit if a command cannot be executed
	-f	Disable wildcards
	-h	Locate functions when defined, not when executed
	-i	Operate in interactive mode
	-k	Place keywords in the environment
	-n	Read-only: read commands but don't execute them
	-p	Do not set effective IDs to actual IDs
	-r	Restricted mode: limit commands and directories
	-s	Take commands from the standard input
	-t	Execute one command and exit
	-u	Cause an error when user attempts to substitute an unset variable
	-v	Display lines of input as they are being read
	-x	Display command lines when executing them

Shell Variables

You can assign a shell variable on any command line, but you usually make assignments in your **.profile** file. Each assignment is of the form *variable=value* (for example, HOME=/usr/paul). Once a shell variable has been assigned, either explicitly or by default, you can invoke it by preceding its name with a dollar sign (for example, $HOME).

CDPATH	Search path for the **cd** command, with individual directory names separated by colons (:). Once CDPATH is set, you can give a relative pathname for a directory listed, and the shell will search the directories for the one intended. For example, with CDPATH=/usr/jeff/admin:/usr/jeff/ltrs:/usr/jeff/test set, you can refer to these directories as simply **admin**, **ltrs**, and **test**.
HOME	Login directory; the **cd** command, without an argument, changes to this directory. For example, suppose you set HOME=/usr/jeff. Then, if you enter the **cd** command without an argument, the shell will move you to **/usr/jeff**, which is often referred to as $HOME.
IFS	Internal field separator (by default, spaces, tabs, and newlines). For example, suppose you set IFS=:. Then the shell will look for colons (instead of spaces, tabs, and newlines) to separate items on a line.
MAIL	Name of mail file. The shell will inform you whenever you receive mail in this file via the **mail** or **mailx** command. For example, suppose you set MAIL=/usr/jeff/admin/mail. Then, each time another user sends you mail, the shell will direct the mail to this file and inform you with the prompt **you have mail**. *See also* **MAILPATH**.
MAILCHECK	Frequency with which the shell checks for mail (by default, 600 seconds, or every 10 minutes). If you set MAILCHECK=1800, the shell will check for mail every half hour. If you set MAILCHECK=0, the shell will check each time it displays its primary prompt on the screen.
MAILPATH	Operates like **MAIL**, except that you can provide a list of mail files, each separated from the next by a colon (:). For example, you could set MAILPATH= :/usr/jeff/admin/mail:/usr/jeff/test/mail. Then the shell will check both files, **/usr/jeff/admin/mail** and **/usr/jeff/test/mail**.

If you want to distinguish mail in one file from mail in another, you can assign to each a separate message. All you have to do is append to the filename a percent sign (%), followed by the message. For example, you could set MAILPATH=:/usr/jeff/admin/mail%you have administrative mail:/usr/jeff/test/mail%you have test mail. Then, if you receive mail in the first file, the shell prompt will be **you have administrative mail**; if you receive mail in the second file, the shell prompt will be **you have test mail**.

PATH
Command file search path. The shell searches the directories listed here for the names of any commands you enter on the command line. For example, suppose you set PATH=:/bin:/usr/bin:$HOME/bin. Then, when you enter a command, the shell will search first in **/bin**, then in **/usr/bin**, then in **$HOME/bin**. (If you have already set HOME=/usr/jeff, the shell will expand the variable and the third directory will be **/usr/jeff/bin**.)

PS1
Primary shell prompt (by default, $). As long as your command lines each occupy a single line, the shell displays only the dollar sign. *See also* **PS2**.

PS2
Secondary shell prompt, used for commands that cannot be completed on a single line (by default, >). The appearance of this prompt indicates that the shell expects more input before the end of the command line. If a command line is too long to fit on a single line, you can force an additional line (along with the secondary shell prompt), by typing a backslash (\) and pressing Enter. For example,

```
$ eqn /usr/pub/eqnchar letters | troff -cm | \
> col | lp
```

The shell reads these two lines as a single line of input. (The backslash at the end of the line makes the shell escape the newline generated when you press Enter.)

SHACCT
Shell accounting file, used to store accounting records for all shell scripts executed. For example, suppose you set SHACCT=/usr/jeff/adm/shell.

Then each time you execute a shell script, the shell will append another accounting record to **/usr/jeff/ adm/shell**.

SHELL   The shell to be used by commands when you escape to a subshell, of particular interest to **vi** and **ed**. The login shell also reads it to determine whether the user should be assigned a restricted shell. For example, you could set SHELL=/usr/lib/rsh to require a user to use the restricted shell.

The restricted shell prevents a user from redirecting output, using files outside the user's home directory, changing directories, or changing the command search path ($PATH).

TERM   Terminal type, required by commands like **vi** that use the entire screen for output. For example, you could set TERM=vt100 to inform the shell that you are using a VT100 terminal.

Input, Output, and Redirection

For each command executed, the shell opens three files: the standard input, the standard output, and the standard error. By default, the standard input is the keyboard, whereas the standard output and standard error are the screen. The shell assigns to each standard file a number called a *file descriptor*. It uses 0, 1, and 2 for standard input, standard output, and standard error; it uses higher numbers, starting at 3, for any other files required to complete the process. *Redirection* means directing output or input to or from a different file.

< *name*   Use *name* as the standard input. For example, with

```
$ mail jan < memo
```

you can mail the contents of **memo** to user jan.

> *name*   Use *name* as the standard output; if *name* doesn't already exist, the shell creates it; if *name* does already exist, the shell overwrites its contents. For example, with

```
$ sort list > list.sort
```

you can sort the contents of **list** and store the output in **list.sort**.

>> *name*   Use *name* as the standard output but append output to it
                if it already exists. For example, with

```
$ sort list >> list.sort
```

you can sort the contents of **list** and append the output
to **list.sort**.

<< [-]*name*   Read input on secondary shell prompts until an input
                line matches *name*, thereby producing a *here document*; if
                the hyphen (-) is used, remove any initial tabs from input
                lines. For example, with this code and output:

```
$ cat - <<STOP
> Begin with this line
> This is the second line
> End with this line
> STOP
Begin with this line
This is the second line
End with this line
$ _
```

you can instruct the shell to continue accepting input
until the string that follows << appears as a line of input.
When that string appears, the document ends and the
command is carried out.

<&*d*   Use file descriptor *d* as the standard input

>&*d*   Use file descriptor *d* as the standard output; usually used
                to save error messages (>&2)

<&-   Close the standard input

>&-   Close the standard output

Grouping and Connecting Commands

The shell offers a number of ways of grouping, listing, and connecting
commands on a command line.

cmd1 | *cmd2*   Pipe: use the output of *cmd1* as the input for *cmd2*

cmd1; *cmd2*   Execute commands *cmd1* and *cmd2* consecutively;
                        the semicolon acts as a command separator

cmd &   Execute command *cmd* in the background

cmd1 && *cmd2*   Execute command *cmd1*; if *cmd1* completes
                        successfully, then execute *cmd2*

cmd1 | | *cmd2*	Execute command *cmd1*; if *cmd1* does not complete successfully, then execute *cmd2*
(*cmd1; cmd2*)	Create a subshell to execute commands *cmd1* and *cmd2*; redirect output of both commands to the same place
{ *cmd1; cmd2;* }	Execute commands *cmd1* and *cmd2* using the current shell

Generating Filenames

Filenames can be generated from the following patterns:

? Match any single character. For example, test.? can represent test.1, test.2, test.a, test.b, or test._.

* Match any string of characters. For example, t*n can represent ten, tin, teen, tern, ton, or turn.

[*list*] Match any single character listed (the list can contain all the characters or show a range of characters). For example, [Bb]est can represent Best or best.

[!*list*] Match any single character not listed. For example, t[!io]n can represent any three letter name but tin or ton.

You can also combine these metacharacters in expressions. For example, [Tt]*n_? can represent Teen_a, turn_1, tan_0, or any of a number of other strings.

Quoting Characters

Removing the special meaning of a character like * is called *quoting* the character. To quote a single character, precede it with a backslash (\). For example, t*t.* can represent test.*, treat.*, or tart.*.

To quote an entire string, enclose the string between a pair of single quotes (' *string* ') or double quotes (" *string* "). Double quotes are similar to single quotes, except that double quotes do not quote the following metacharacters:

- dollar sign ($)
- back quotes (' *command* ')
- backslash (\).

Therefore, double quotes are better suited for expressions that contain shell variables (which begin with $) and command substitutions (which use ' and ').

Logical Constructions

The shell enables you to branch to another line of your shell program with the **if** and **case** statements. The shell also enables you to construct loops with the **while**, **until**, and **for** statements.

Single Branching

```
if expression
   then command list
fi
```

For example, consider the following pair of shell scripts:

```
$ cat disp
if true
   then echo 'DISPLAY THIS'
fi
$ disp
DISPLAY THIS
$ _
```

The shell statement **true** forces the **then** statement to be executed. Therefore, the words are displayed on the screen.

```
$ cat trial
if false
   then echo 'DISPLAY THIS'
fi
$ trial
$ _
```

The shell statement **false** prevents the **then** statement from being executed. Therefore, the text is not displayed.

```
if expression
   then command list 1
else command list 2
fi
```

For example, consider the following short shell script called **compare**:

```
$ cat compare
if c='expr "comparison" : "$1"'
   then echo " $c characters agree "
```

```
else echo 'No characters in common'
fi
$ _
```

To use this shell script, you have to enter its name followed by a string ($1). The shell compares the string you enter with the word comparison; then the shell assigns the number of consecutive characters matched to variable c. If any characters match, c is assigned a value equal to at least one (indicating true); if no characters match, c is assigned the value zero (indicating false). Here are two uses of **compare**:

```
$ compare compute
4 characters agree
$ _
```

In the first instance, the letters **comp** match and c is assigned the value 4, the number of matching letters. The shell substitutes 4 into the output. Because the value isn't zero, the expression is true and the shell executes the **then** statement.

```
$ compare zero
No characters in common
$ _
```

In the second instance, no characters match and c is assigned the value 0. Because the expression is false, the shell executes the **else** statement.

Multiple Branching

Branch to the command list that is prefaced by an expression that matches the *string*. The expressions *s1*, *s2*, *s3*, and so on, can be any alphanumeric combinations you choose. They can be single letters, numbers, or words. To allow more than one choice, you can separate each choice from the next with an OR symbol (|).

```
case string in
   s1) command list 1 ;;
   s2) command list 2 ;;
   s3) command list 3 ;;
   ...
   sn) command list n ;;
esac
```

The **case** statement often follows the selection of a choice. A user typically selects an item from a menu. The choice the user makes determines what the shell script does next. Here is an example:

```
echo '        EDITING MENU\n\n        '
echo '1  Change to directory        D or d'
echo '2  Edit                       E or e'
echo '3  Format                     F or f'
echo '4  Exit                       X or x'
echo '   Enter your selection: \c            '
       read choice
```

The preceding lines will display the following on the screen:

```
        EDITING MENU
1  Change to directory        D or d
2  Edit                       E or e
3  Format                     F or f
4  Exit                       X or x
   Enter your selection: _
```

The menu just shown displays four possible selections, with three ways of making each selection. For example, to change to a new directory, the user can enter 1, D, or d. The **read choice** statement at the end of the menu script stores the user's response in a variable called **choice**. Now the **case** statement begins:

```
case $choice in
   1|D|d) echo 'Name of the new directory: \c'
            read dir; cd $dir ;;
   2|E|e) echo 'Name of document to edit: \c'
            read doc; vi $doc ;;
   3|F|f) echo 'Name of document to format: \c'
            read doc; ... ;;
   4|X|x) echo 'You are leaving the Editing Menu' ;;
   *)       echo 'Enter D, E, F, or X' ;;
esac
```

If the user entered 1, D, or d in response to the menu prompt just described, the shell now executes the first branch (change directory). The shell prompts for a directory name, stores the name in $dir, and makes the change.

If the user entered 2, E, or e, the shell executes the second branch (edit a document).

If the user entered 3, F, or f, the shell executes the third branch (format a document; if the user entered 4, X, or x, the shell executes the fourth branch (exit from this menu).

If the user entered any other number or letter, the fifth branch reprompts the user, repeating the valid choices. The **case** statement always ends with **esac**, which is "case" spelled backward.

You must terminate each branch with a pair of semicolons (;;), which means you can use single semicolons (;) within the branch, as illustrated in the **case** statement example.

Forming Loops

```
while command list 1          Loop while true
   do command list 2
done
```

A simple example of a **while** loop follows:

```
i=5
while i='expr $i - 1'
do echo Counter is $i
done
```

The output of this loop will be the following:

```
Counter is 4
Counter is 3
Counter is 2
Counter is 1
```

The counter is initialized to 5. On the first iteration, it is decremented to 4 and displayed. It is then decremented on each subsequent iteration until its value is 1. On the fifth iteration, the counter becomes zero and the loop ends.

```
until command list 1          Loop while false
   do command list 2
done
```

A simple example of an **until** loop follows:

```
i=1
until i='expr $i - 1'
do echo Counter is $i
done
```

The output of this loop will be the following:

```
Counter is 0
```

The counter is initialized to 1. On the first iteration, it is decremented to 0 and displayed. It is then decremented to -1 (a nonzero value) on the second iteration and the loop ends.

```
for variable in list          Loop on variable
   do command list
done
```

The **for** statement relies on a list of words, which can be either numbers or strings. Here is a simple example:

```
ingred='apple berry cake dough'
for word in $ingred
   do echo $ingred
done
```

The output of the sample shell script is the following:

```
apple
berry
cake
dough
```

On each iteration, the shell selects another word from the list of words and displays it on the screen.

An alternate way to use the **for** statement is to generate a list from a UNIX command. Here is an example:

```
set 'ls'
for file
   do echo $file
done
```

The output will be a list of the files in the current directory, generated by the **ls** command. When you use the **for** statement in this way, the **in** *list* statement becomes unnecessary. The following is equivalent to the previous shell script:

```
for file in *
 _do echo $file
done
```

In the example, the asterisk (*) is replaced with the names of the files in the current directory.

Defining a Function

You can assign any list of commands to a function name by using the format

```
name () { command list; }
```

For a function of any length, the format usually looks like this:

```
name ()
{
    command list
}
```

Here is a simple example of a function:

```
rename ()
{
    echo "Current name: \c"
    read file
    echo "Desired name: \c"
    read change
    mv $file $change
    echo "File $file has been renamed $change \n"
}
```

This function renames a file with a short interactive dialog. Here is an example of using this function:

```
$ rename
Current name: complicated
Desired name: simple
File complicated has been renamed simple
$ _
```

The shell prompts you for the old name first, then the new name. Then it changes the name with the **mv** command. The shell function is very short and simple. For a real-life function that you use on your system, you would want to incorporate safeguards into your function. For example, you would want to make sure that the target filename doesn't already exist.

Testing Files

The previous example of a function raised the issue of testing files. The shell offers you five different file tests:

[-r name]   File *name* exists and can be read
[-w name]   File *name* exists and can be written to
[-f name]   File *name* exists and is a regular file
[-d name]   File *name* exists and is a directory
[-s name]   File *name* exists and is not empty

You could use one of these tests to enhance the **rename** function described earlier.

```
rename ()
{
```

```
echo "Current name: \c"
read file
echo "Desired name: \c"
read FILE
if [ -f $FILE ]
   then echo "$FILE already exists"
   else mv $file $FILE
   echo "File $file has been renamed $FILE \n"
fi
}
```

Comparing Quantities

The shell enables you to perform any of six comparisons between two numerical quantities:

```
[ X -eq Y ]    Is X equal to Y?
[ X -ne Y ]    Is X not equal to Y?
[ X -lt Y ]    Is X less than Y?
[ X -le Y ]    Is X less than or equal to Y?
[ X -gt Y ]    Is X greater than Y?
[ X -ge Y ]    Is X greater than or equal to Y?
```

For example, suppose **$min** is the minimum size you are looking for and **$size** is the size of the current file (called **$name**). You could test to determine whether the current file is the minimum size by using a script like the following:

```
min=20000
for name in *
   do size='wc -c < $name'
   if [ $size -ge $min ]
      then echo "$name is a large file: $size characters"
   fi
done
```

This shell script shown scans the current directory for large files (at least 20,000 characters long). Each time it finds one, it displays the name of the file and its length in characters. The **if** statement makes the actual comparison, testing the size of the current file against the minimum size.

Comparing Strings

The shell can test strings also, using one of four different tests:

```
[ -n string ]    Does the string exist?
[ -z string ]    Does the string not exist?
```

```
[ s1 = s2 ]              Are the two strings the same?
[ s1 != s2 ]             Are the two strings not the same?
```

In the second test just shown, -z is equivalent to !-n. In the first test shown, you can omit -n. You can test for the existence of a string in one of two ways:

```
if [ -n "$1" ]
```

or

```
if [ "$1" ]
```

You can also test for the nonexistence of a string in one of two ways:

```
if [ !-n "$1" ]
```

or

```
if [ -z "$1" ]
```

The double quotes are used in the examples to retain the meanings of special characters and treat spaces as characters. If you want the shell to disregard spaces, you can omit the double quotes, as shown here:

```
if [ $first = $third ]
```

This example will be true if the two variables are identical or even if they are the same except for spaces. For example, they could be assigned the following values and still be identical:

```
first=' train'
third=train
```

As shown, the equal sign used in an assignment statement can be entered without a space on each side. However, when an equal sign (or a not equal sign) is used in a comparison, it must be preceded and followed by a space. For example, you must enter

```
if [ $first = $third ]
```

not

```
if [ $first=$third ]              [not acceptable ]
```

Compound Testing

To perform compound testing of files, quantities, or strings, you can use the following logical operators:

```
-a   AND:  True only if both statements are true
-o   OR:   True if either statement is true
!    NOT:  True becomes false; false becomes true
```

For example,

```
if [ ! false ]
```

is equivalent to

```
if [ true ]
```

The statement

```
if [ -f $name -a -r $name -o -w $name ]
```

checks whether a file called **name** exists and is either readable or writable by the owner of the shell script.

Command Substitution and Parameters

Command substitution means replacing a command with its output:

```
name=`command`
```

For example, you could use the following in a shell script:

```
list=`ls`
```

The effect of this command is to assign to a variable **list** the names of the files in the current directory. If the directory contains five files called **art**, **cut**, **head**, **foot**, and **text**, the **list** statement is equivalent to the following:

```
list=`art cut head foot text`
```

Another way to use this kind of statement is as follows:

```
i=4
while i=`expr $i - 1`
   do echo $i
done
```

The initial value of the counter (i) is 4. The assignment that follows **while** reduces the value of i to 3 on the first iteration, then to 2, then to 1, then to 0, which ends the loop. The back quotes allow the **expr** statement to generate a new value for i. The value generated runs the loop through three iterations and also provides a mechanism for ending the loop.

The positional parameters represent the command and its arguments on the command line:

```
$0    The command itself
$1    The first argument
$2    The second argument
$3    The third argument (and so on, up to 9)
```

177

For example, the **date** command generates five arguments:

```
$ date
Thu Mar 25 15:08:19 1994
$ _
```

In this example, $1 is Thu, $2 is Mar, $3 is 25, $4 is 15:08:19, and $5 is 1994. By using the **set** command, you can assign the positional parameters for subsequent use, as follows:

```
$ set 'date'
$ echo "$5 \n"
1994
$ _
```

Here the **echo** command displays only the fifth argument of the **date** command, the year. You can also use positional parameters to rearrange the output of a command:

```
$ echo 'Today is $1, $2 $3, $4 at $5 /n'
Today is Thu, Mar 25, 1994 at 15:08:19
$ _
```

There are two ways to name a shell variable called *var*:

$var   Name variable *var*

${var}   Name variable *var*, with allowance for embedding in a string

For example, you could embed one string into another in the following way:

```
$ c=communica
$ t=tele{$c}tions
$ echo $t \n
telecommunications
$ _
```

In this example, the shell embeds the string **c** (communica) into the string **t**, which begins with tele and ends with tions.

Conditional substitution enables you to make assignments depending on prior assignment of values:

${var:-string}   If *var* has been assigned a value, then the value of this expression is $*var*; otherwise, it is $*string*

Here is an example, with one variable assigned and one left unassigned:

```
$ fruit=pear
$ veg=
$ echo ${fruit:-apple} with ${veg:-carrot}
```

```
pear with carrot
$ _
```

As another example, suppose you want to make a backup copy of a file. Suppose further that you want to have the option of naming a particular target directory. It is understood that if you don't name the directory, then the backup copy will be placed in the current directory. Then you could use something like the following in a shell script called **backup**:

```
file=$1
dir=${2:-.}
cp $file $dir/{$file}_bak
```

As this partial shell script indicates, you must name the file to be backed up as the first argument ($1), but you don't necessarily have to name the target directory as the second argument ($2). So you can enter **backup** in one of two ways:

```
$ backup test
```

Use this **backup** command line to make a backup copy of **test**, called **test_bak**, in the current directory.

```
$ backup test $HOME/archive
```

Use the preceding command line to make a backup copy of **test**, called **test_bak**, in a subdirectory of your login directory called **archive**.

${*var*:=*string*}   Same as the previous command, except that the shell also assigns the value of *string* to *var*

To use the **backup** example introduced above again, you could use the following lines:

```
file=$1
dir=$2
echo Target directory is ${dir:='pwd'}
cp $file $dir/{$file}_bak
```

If the name of the target directory is entered on the command line as the second argument ($2), that directory is the name used. If no name is entered, the shell assigns the name of the current directory and that is the name used.

${*var*:+*string*}   If *var* has been assigned a value, the value of this expression is $*string*; otherwise, it is null and the value of *var* remains unassigned

For example, suppose you have a variable called MSG that determines whether to display a message on the screen. If MSG is unassigned, there is no message; if MSG is assigned, there is a message, but it will be the message shown here. In this way, one variable can control what happens on many different lines of your shell script:

```
echo ${MSG:+'Incorrect specification entered\n'}
```

If MSG has been assigned a value, the shell displays the message **Incorrect specification entered** here; if MSG has not been assigned a value, no message appears.

${*var*?*string*}   If *var* has been assigned a value, the value of this expression is $*var*; otherwise, the program displays a message and exits

For example, consider the following:

```
$ OK='No problem here'
$ echo ${OK:nok} \n
No problem here
$ _
```

Because the variable OK has an assigned value, that value is displayed and processing continues.

But suppose variable OK is unassigned, as shown here:

```
$ nok='Variable not set — abort'
$ echo ${OK:nok} \n
test: OK: Variable not set — abort
$ _
```

Because variable OK has no assigned value, the shell displays the value of variable nok and aborts immediately.

Reserved Shell Variables

The following shell variables provide system information:

$#   Number of arguments in a command line

For example, suppose we check the **date** command again:

```
$ set 'date'
$ echo $# \n
5
$ _
```

The shell responds by displaying 5, the number of arguments output by the **date** command.

$?   Return code for a command

```
$ date
Thu Mar 25 15:08:19 1994
$ echo "$? \n"
0
$ _
```

The return code is zero, meaning the process was executed successfully. A nonzero return code means an error in execution.

$$ PID of the current process

Because the process ID of each process is unique, it is sometimes used in the name of a temporary file. Here is an example:

```
$ tmp=sort$$
$ sort table > $tmp
$ mv $tmp table
$ _
```

In this example, we needed a place to store the output of the **sort** command. The name we chose was **sort**, followed by the process ID of the **sort** command.

$!   PID of the most recent background process

You can use this variable to recall the process ID, as shown here:

```
$ echo "$! \n"
1073
$ _
```

With the number recalled, you can kill the process if necessary.

$-   Status of shell flags

You can use this variable to display which flags are currently set, as shown here:

```
$ echo "$- \n"
e
$ _
```

Only the e (exit) flag is set. See the **set** command later in this appendix.

Built-In Shell Commands

You can use any of the following commands without starting a new shell.

:	Null command: The shell performs no action and returns an execution code of zero (same as **true**)
. *file*	Execute the commands in *file* as part of the current process
break [*n*]	Exit from *n* levels of a **for** or **while** loop (by default, one level)
cd [*directory*]	Change to *directory* indicated (by default **$HOME**)
continue [*n*]	Skip the rest of the current **for** or **while** loop and resume execution with the next iteration of the loop that is nested *n*-1 levels above the current loop (by default, the current loop)
echo *arg(s)*	Echo arguments (display on the screen)
eval [*arg(s)*]	Execute the arguments provided, allowing evaluation and substitution of shell variables
exec [*arg(s)*]	Execute the arguments provided without starting a new process
exit [*n*]	Exit from the current shell procedure with an exit value of *n*
export [*name(s)*]	Export the parameter(s) named to the environment of any commands subsequently executed; display exported variables
getopts *string var* [*arg(s)*]	Check command options, using two mandatory arguments and one optional:
	string List of valid option letters, followed by a colon (:) if the option has an argument of its own
	var Variable in which to store the next option

	arg(s)	Check the arguments provided instead of the command line
hash [-r] [*name(s)*]		Set up a tracked alias for a command, thereby speeding up execution; clear tracked aliases with the **-r** option
newgrp [-] [*group*]		Switch to *group*; if **-** is used, start with your login environment
pwd		Display the path name of the current working directory
read [*name(s)*]		Read from the standard input and assign input to the name(s) provided
readonly [*name(s)*]		Make the variables named read-only, thereby prohibiting further assignment
return [*n*]		Exit from a function with exit status *n* and return to the shell
set [*flag(s)[arg(s)]*]		Assign arguments *arg(s)* to the positional parameters; activate (-) or deactivate (+) *flag(s)* (from the following list) that affects the operation of the current shell; display the names and values of shell variables, along with the names and definitions of functions
	-/+a	Export/do not export variables that are created or modified
	-/+e	Exit/do not exit if a command exits with a nonzero (error) exit status
	-/+f	Disable/enable generation of filenames from wildcards
	-/+h	Hashing: Provide/do not provide quick access to commands used in a function
	-/+k	Keyword arguments: Provide/do not provide all keyword arguments (shell variables) for a command
	-/+n	Read but do not execute/execute commands
	-/+t	Execute/do not execute one command and exit

183

	-/+u	Cause/do not cause an error when attempting to substitute for an unset variable
	-/+v	Display/do not display input lines
	-/+x	Display/do not display command lines after they are ready for execution
shift [*n*]		Shift positional parameters *n* places (by default, one place) to the left
test		Test conditional expressions and set to true or false; use either the **test** command or a pair of brackets
times		Display cumulative user and system time for all processes run by the shell
trap [*cmd(s)*][*s*]		Trap signal number *s* and execute *cmd(s)*; if *s*=0, execute *cmd(s)* when the shell exits; if *cmd(s)* and *s* are omitted, display the commands currently being executed and the signal numbers currently being trapped
type [*name(s)*]		Display the full pathname of the command(s) named
ulimit [-f *b*]		Set a limit of *b* blocks for files created by the shell and its child processes; if the -f *b* option is omitted, display the current limit
umask [*mmm*]		Set the user creation mask *mmm*, which establishes permissions for new files created; if *mmm* is omitted, display the current user creation mask
unset [*name(s)*]		Unset the functions and variables named
wait [*n*]		Wait for process with PID *n* to complete in the background and display its exit status

C

The C Shell

Appendix C summarizes the command processor developed at the University of California during the 1970s, which is known as the C shell. The C shell, named after the C programming language, provides many enhancements to the Bourne shell, including the ability to reexecute commands, alias commands, define functions, substitute variables in more ways, and evaluate arithmetic expressions in more ways.

```
% csh [option(s)] [argument(s)]
```

Options

	-b	Break option processing
	-c *string*	Read commands from *string*, which is usually the name of a file that contains a shell script
	-e	Exit if a command fails
	-f	Do not execute **.cshrc** (for faster start)
	-i	Operate in interactive mode
	-n	Read only: Read commands but don't execute them
	-s	Take commands from the standard input
	-t	Execute one command and exit
	-v	Verbose: Display input lines while reading them
	-V	Set **-v** before reading **.cshrc**
	-x	Debug: Display command lines, preceded by plus signs (+), when executing them
	-X	Set **-x** before reading **.cshrc**

Shell Variables

You can assign a shell variable on any command line, but you usually make assignments in one of the following files:

- `$HOME/.cshrc`
- `/etc/login`
- `$HOME/.login`

Each assignment is of the form *variable=value* (for example, HOME= /usr/paul). Once a shell variable has been assigned—either explicitly or by default—you can invoke it by preceding its name with a dollar sign (for example, $HOME). The C shell sets each capitalized variable at login; then the C shell resets it each time the user resets the corresponding lowercase variable.

cdpath   Search path for the **cd** command, with individual directory names separated by spaces. Once CDPATH is set, you can give a relative pathname for a directory listed; then the shell will search the directories for the one intended. For example, with CDPATH= (/usr/jeff/admin /usr/jeff/ltrs /usr/jeff/test) set, you can refer to these directories as simply **admin**, **ltrs**, and **test**.

echo   Echo (display) each command with all substitutions in place for execution

fignore   A list of suffixes to filenames for the shell to ignore when it is completing filenames (often, fignore=.o)

filec   Enable completion of filenames, using two special key combinations:

    Ctrl+D Display filenames that begin with the string just entered

    Esc Replace the string just entered with the longest extension possible

hardpaths   Force all pathnames to contain only actual directory names, without symbolic links

histchars   A two-character string that includes the history substitution character (by default, !) and the quick substitution character (^)

history   The number of command lines allowed for the history file (typically around 100–200)

HOME   Login directory; the **cd** command, without an argument, changes to this directory. (The tilde (~) also refers to this directory.) For example, suppose you set HOME= /usr/jeff. Then, if you enter the **cd** command without an argument, the shell moves you to **/usr/jeff**, which is often referred to as $HOME.

ignoreeof	Force the shell to ignore the EOF character (Ctrl+D) when typed at the keyboard
mail	A list of mail files; if the list begins with a number, **m**, the shell must check the mail files every **m** minutes. For example, you could set mail=(/usr/jeff/admin/mail /usr/jeff/test/mail). Then the shell will check both files, **/usr/jeff/admin/mail** and **/usr/jeff/test/mail**.
nobeep	Turn off terminal beeping while completing ambiguous filenames
noglob	Prevent substitution of filenames
nonomatch	Return the pattern for expanding a filename instead of an error if the shell cannot match any actual filenames
notify	Force the shell to notify you as soon as a job completes
PATH (path)	Command file search path. The shell searches the directories listed here for the names of any commands you enter on the command line. For example, suppose you set path=(/bin /usr/bin $HOME/bin). Then, when you enter a command, the shell searches first in **/bin**, then in **/usr/bin**, then in **$HOME/bin**. (If you have already set HOME=/usr/jeff, the shell expands the variable and the third directory will be **/usr/jeff/bin**.)
prompt	The primary shell prompt (by default, %) displayed on the screen each time the shell is prepared to accept new input
savehist	The number of lines to be saved in the .history file when you log out; the higher the number, the longer the C shell takes to log in
shell	The shell to be used by commands when you escape to a subshell, of particular interest to **vi** and **ed**. The login shell also reads it to determine whether the user should be assigned a restricted shell. For example, you could set SHELL=/usr/lib/rcsh to require a user to use the restricted shell.

The restricted shell prevents a user from redirecting output, using files outside the user's home directory, changing directories, or changing the command search path ($PATH).

TERM (term) Terminal type, required by commands like **vi** that use the entire screen for output. For example, you could set TERM=vt100 to inform the shell that you are using a VT100 terminal.

USER (user) The name of the user who owns the current shell

verbose Display each command line after a history substitution

Input, Output, and Redirection

For each command executed, the shell opens three files, which are called the standard input, the standard output, and the standard error. By default, the standard input is the keyboard, and the standard output and standard error are the video screen. The shell assigns to each standard file a number called a *file descriptor*. The descriptor uses 0, 1, and 2 for standard input, standard output, and standard error; it uses higher numbers, starting at 3, for any other files required to complete the process. *Redirection* means directing output to or input from a different file.

< *name* Use *name* as the standard input. For example, with

```
% mail jan < memo
```

you can mail the contents of **memo** to user jan.

> *name* Use *name* as the standard output; if *name* doesn't already exist, the shell creates it; if *name* does already exist, the shell overwrites its contents. For example, with

```
% sort list > list.sort
```

you can sort the contents of **list** and store the output in **list.sort**.

>> *name* Use *name* as the standard output, but append output to it if it already exists. For example, with

```
% sort list >> list.sort
```

you can sort the contents of **list** and append the output to **list.sort**.

<< [-]*name*   Read input on secondary shell prompts until an input line matches *name*, thereby producing a *here document*; if the hyphen (-) is used, remove any initial tabs from input lines. For example, with

```
% cat - <<STOP
> Begin with this line
> This is the second line
> End with this line
> STOP
Begin with this line
This is the second line
End with this line
% _
```

you can instruct the shell to continue accepting input until the string that follows << appears as a line of input. When that string appears, the document ends and the command is carried out.

<&*d*   Use file descriptor *d* as the standard input

>&*d*   Use file descriptor *d* as the standard output, usually used to save error messages (>&2)

<&-   Close the standard input

>&-   Close the standard output

Grouping and Connecting Commands

The shell offers a number of ways of grouping, listing, and connecting commands on a command line.

cmd1 | cmd2   Use the ouput of **cmd1** as the input for **cmd2**

cmd1; cmd2   Execute commands **cmd1** and **cmd2** consecutively

cmd &   Execute command **cmd** in the background

cmd1 && cmd2   Execute command **cmd1**; if **cmd1** completes successfully, execute **cmd2**

cmd1 || cmd2   Execute command **cmd1**; if **cmd1** does not complete successfully, execute **cmd2**

(cmd1; cmd2)   Create a subshell to execute commands **cmd1** and **cmd2**

{ cmd1; cmd2; }   Execute commands **cmd1** and **cmd2** using the current shell

Generating Filenames

Filenames can be generated from the following patterns:

?   Match any single character. For example, test.? can represent test.1, test.2, test.a, test.b, or test._.

*   Match any string of characters. For example, t*n can represent ten, tin, teen, tern, or turn.

[*list*]   Match any single character listed (the list can contain all the characters or show a range of characters). For example, [Bb]est can represent Best or best.

[!*list*]   Match any single character not listed. For example, t[!io]n can represent anything but tin or ton.

You can also combine these metacharacters in expressions. For example, [Tt]*n_? can represent Teen_a, turn_1, tan_0, or any of a number of other strings.

Quoting Characters

Removing the special meaning of a character like * is called *quoting* the character. To quote a single character, precede it with a backslash (\). For example, t*t.* can represent test.*, treat.*, or tart.*.

To quote an entire string, use one of the following pairs of symbols:

* Single quotes   Interpret metacharacters literally

* Double quotes   Interpret metacharacters symbolically

* Parentheses   Interpret metacharacters symbolically and form an array

Using the History File

You can set up automatic line numbering for your prompts by inserting an exclamation point (!). For example, if you place the line

```
set prompt="[!] "
```

in your **$HOME/.cshr** file, it will display the following prompts when you begin work:

```
[1] _
[2] _
[3] _
. . .
```

Because the exclamation point has a special meaning in the C shell, you have to escape the exclamation point (\!) any time you use it for any purpose other than specifying an event.

Another line you can place in your **$HOME/.cshr** file is one like the following:

```
set history = 50
```

The effect of this line is to maintain a history file of the previous 50 events, or command lines that you have entered. You now can access any of these events for quick recall and reentry. To display a list of the events in your history file, enter the following command line:

```
[10] history
```

You can recall and execute events in your history file by using the following symbols. The C shell will first display the command line and then its output.

!!   Reinvoke the most recent event. For example:

```
[11] cat letter
. . .
[12] !!
cat letter
. . .
[13] _
```

!*n*   Reinvoke event number *n*. For example:

```
[13] !11
cat letter
. . .
[14] _
```

!-*i*   Reinvoke the event that is *i* lines prior to the current event.
         For example:

```
[14] !-3
cat letter
...
[15] _
```

!*x*   Reinvoke the most recent event that begins with character *x*.
         For example:

```
[15] !c
cat letter
...
[16] _
```

!?*x*   Reinvoke the event that contains character *x* anywhere on the
         line. For example:

```
[16] !?i
history
...
[17] _
```

With the following symbols, you can select individual
arguments from an event in the history file. To illustrate,
examine the following sample command line:

```
[17] echo arg1 arg2 arg3 arg4 arg5
arg1 arg2 arg3 arg4 arg5
[18] _
```

!*n*:*a*   Select argument *a* from event *n*. For example:

```
[18] echo !!:3
echo arg3
arg3
[19] _
```

!*n*:*a-b* Select arguments *a-b* from event *n*. For example:

```
[19] echo 17:2-4
echo arg2 arg3 arg4
arg2 arg3 arg4
[20] _
```

!*n*:^   Select the first argument.

!*n*^   Select the first argument. For example:

```
[20] echo !17:^
echo arg1
arg1
[21] _
```

!*n*:$ Select the last argument.

!*n*$ Select the last argument. For example:

```
[21] echo !17:$
echo arg5
arg5
[22] _
```

!*n*:*   Select all arguments.

!*n**   Select all arguments. For example:

```
[22] echo !17:*
echo arg1 arg2 arg3 arg4 arg5
arg1 arg2 arg3 arg4 arg5
[23] _
```

With the three commands just shown, you can omit the colon
(:).

You can use the following symbols to make substitutions in an event
before reexecuting it:

!*n*:s/*word1*/*word2*   Substitute: Replace *word1* with *word2* (first
occurrence only). For example:

```
[23] echo !17:s/a/A
echo Arg1 arg2 arg3 arg4 arg5
Arg1 arg2 arg3 arg4 arg5
[24] _
```

!*n*:i:s/*word1*/*word2*   Substitute: Replace *word1* with *word2* (*i*th word
only). For example:

```
[24] echo !17:5:s/a/A
echo Arg5
Arg5
[25] _
```

!*n*:gs/*word1*/*word2*   Global substitute: replace *word1* with *word2*
(every occurrence). For example:

```
[25] echo !17:gs/w/W
echo Arg1 Arg2 Arg3 Arg4 Arg5
Arg1 Arg2 Arg3 Arg4 Arg5
[26] _
```

!*n*:&   Repeat the previous substitution. For this example, return to command line 24:

```
[23] echo !17:s/a/A
echo Arg1 arg2 arg3 arg4 arg5
Arg1 arg2 arg3 arg4 arg5
[24] echo !!:&
echo Arg1 Arg2 arg3 arg4 arg5
Arg1 Arg2 arg3 arg4 arg5
[25] _
```

You can use the following symbols to modify a pathname in an event in the history file. To understand these symbols, consider the following sample command line:

```
[30] echo /usr/jeff/adm/report.bak
/usr/jeff/adm/report.bak
[31] _
```

!*n*:h   Head: Remove the last name from a pathname. For example:

```
[31] echo !!:h
echo /usr/jeff/adm
/usr/jeff/adm
[32] _
```

!*n*:t   Tail: Remove the prefix from a pathname. For example:

```
[32] echo !30:t
echo report.bak
report.bak
[33] _
```

!*n*:r   Remove the suffix from a pathname. For example:

```
[33] echo !30:r
echo /usr/jeff/adm/report
/usr/jeff/adm/report
[34] _
```

You can use the following symbols to perform other functions on events in the history file:

!*n*:p   Print: Preview a command line without executing it. For example:

```
[34] echo !30:p
echo /usr/jeff/adm/report.bak
[35] _
```

!*n*:q   Quote: Protect a command line from further
             modification. For example:

```
[35] echo !30:q
echo /usr/jeff/adm/report.bak
/usr/jeff/adm/report.bak
[36] _
```

Using Aliases

The C shell supports *aliases*, which are substitute names for command
lines. As with prompt and history information, you can store aliases in
your **$HOME/.cshrc** file. You can set up a new alias with the **alias**
command or remove an existing one with the **unalias** command. If you
enter the **alias** command without an argument, it displays the aliases
currently in effect, as shown here:

```
[40] alias
alias s1 vi /usr/jeff/pubs/section_1
alias s2 vi /usr/jeff/pubs/section_2
alias s3 vi /usr/jeff/pubs/section_3
alias s4 vi /usr/jeff/pubs/section_4
alias s5 vi /usr/jeff/pubs/section_5
[41] _
```

The purpose of each alias is to enable you to enter a short command line
like **s3** instead of a long command line like **vi /usr/jeff/pubs/section_3**.

You can allow for a dynamic selection by setting up the alias in the
following way:

```
alias ss vi /usr/jeff/pubs/section_\!*
```

With this alias set up, either on a command line or in your **$HOME/.cshrc**
file, you are now free to enter a command line like the following:

```
[41] ss 4
```

instead of

```
[41] vi /usr/jeff/pubs/section_4
```

You can combine several commands in a single alias, as long as you
quote special symbols. Here is an example:

```
alias clp 'cd \!*; ls -l | page'
```

195

With this alias set up, either on a command line or in your **$HOME/.cshrc** file, you can now enter a command line like the following:

```
[42] clp ../adm
```

The effect of this command line is to execute the following command lines in succession:

```
cd ../adm
ls -l | page
```

The C shell first changes to the directory named, then displays a long listing of the files in that directory, piped to the **page** command to allow for easy viewing.

Finally, you can assign aliases recursively to as many levels as necessary. Here is an example:

```
[43] alias abc def
[44] alias def ghi
[45] alias ghi clp
[46] abc /usr/jane/adm/tools
```

The effect of command line 46 is to invoke the alias **clp** with the argument **/usr/jan/adm/tools**.

Using String Variables

The **set** command enables you to assign a value to a string variable, for example, **set prompt="[!] "** or **set history=50**. To display all variables currently declared, along with their assigned values, enter **set** on a command line by itself.

The C shell allows you to treat the string value of any variable as an array, as long as the value was originally assigned within a pair of parentheses. For example, consider the following assignment:

```
set path=(/etc/bin /bin /usr/bin /usr/jeff/bin .)
```

Variable **path** is an array with five elements. You can use bracketed subscripts to denote the individual elements:

```
[51] echo $path[1]
/etc/bin
[52] echo $path[2]
/bin
```

```
[53] echo $path[3]
/usr/bin
[54] echo $path[4]
/usr/jeff/bin
[55] echo $path[5]
.
[56] _
```

Two C shell variables can be useful in finding information about variables:

- **?** Has the variable been declared? (One means yes; zero means no.) For example:

  ```
  [56] echo $#path
  1
  [57] _
  ```

- **#** How many elements does the array contain? For example:

  ```
  [57] echo $#path
  5
  [58] _
  ```

Using Numeric Variables

The C shell uses the @ command instead of **set** to assign values to numeric variables. As with the **set** command, you can enter @ by itself on a command line to display the current settings:

```
[60] @
a       15
b       3
i       10
j       24
[61] _
```

The @ command, used with the following operators, replaces the **expr** command of the Bourne shell:

+ Addition
- Subtraction
* Multiplication
/ Division
% Remainder

Here are a few examples:

```
[61] @ x = 5
[62] @ y = $x + 7
[63] @ z = $y / 2
[64] echo $x $y $z
5 12 6
[65] _
```

Other operators used by the C shell are as follows:

++	Increase the value by one
+=*n*	Increase the value by *n*
--	Decrease the value by one
-=*n*	Decrease the value by *n*
=~	Obtain the one's complement

Logical Constructions

The shell enables you to branch to another line of your shell program with the **if** and **switch** statements. The C shell also enables you to construct loops with the **while, until,** and **foreach** statements.

Single Branching

```
if expression then
            command list
endif
```

For example, consider the following pair of shell scripts:

```
% cat disp
if -e disp then
   echo 'DISPLAY THIS'
endif
% disp
DISPLAY THIS
% _
```

The C shell statement : forces the **then** statement to be executed. Therefore, the words are displayed on the screen.

```
% cat trial
if -z trial then
   echo 'DISPLAY THIS'
```

```
endif
% trial
% _
```

The C shell statement **false** prevents the **then** statement from being executed. Therefore, the text is not displayed.

```
if expression then
   command list 1
else
   command list 2
endif
```

For example, consider the following short shell script called **compare**:

```
% cat compare
if (c='expr "comparison" : "$1"') then
   echo " $c characters agree "
else
   echo 'No characters in common'
endif
% _
```

To use this shell script, you have to enter its name followed by a string ($1). The shell compares the string you enter with the word comparison; then the shell assigns the number of consecutive characters matched to variable c. If any characters match, c is assigned a value equal to at least one (indicating true); if no characters match, c is assigned the value zero (indicating false). Here are two uses of **compare**:

```
% compare compute
4 characters agree
% _
```

In the first instance, the letters **comp** match and c is assigned the value 4, the number of matching letters. The shell substitutes 4 into the output. Because the value isn't zero, the expression is true and the shell executes the **then** statement.

```
% compare zero
No characters in common
% _
```

In the second instance, no characters match and c is assigned the value 0. Because the expression is false, the shell executes the **else** statement.

Multiple Branching

Branch to the command list that is prefaced by a pattern that matches the *string*. The patterns *pattern1, pattern2, pattern3,* and so on, can be any alphanumeric combinations you choose. They can be single letters, numbers, or words.

```
switch (string)
case pattern1:
  command list 1
breaksw
case pattern2:
  command list 2
breaksw
case pattern3:
  command list 3
breaksw
default:                      [optional]
  command list
breaksw
endsw
```

The **switch** statement often follows the selection of a choice. A user typically selects an item from a menu. The choice the user makes determines what the shell script does next. Here is an example:

```
echo '    EDITING MENU\n\n              '
echo '1   Change to directory       D or d'
echo '2   Edit                      E or e'
echo '3   Format                    F or f'
echo '4   Exit                      X or x'
echo '    Enter your selection: \c         '
set choice=$<
```

The preceding lines will display the following on the screen:

```
EDITING MENU
1 Change to directory       D or d
2 Edit                      E or e
3 Format                    F or f
4 Exit                      X or x
  Enter your selection: _
```

The menu displays four possible selections, with three ways of making each selection. For example, to change to a new directory, the user can enter 1, D, or d. The **read choice** statement at the end of the menu script above stores the user's response in a variable called **choice**. Now the **switch** statement begins:

```
switch ($choice)
  case 1|D|d:
    echo 'Name of the new directory: \c'
    read dir; cd $dir
  breaksw
  case 2|E|e:
    echo 'Name of document to edit: \c'
    read doc; vi $doc
  breaksw
  case 3|F|f:
    echo 'Name of document to format: \c'
    read doc; ...
  breaksw
  case 4|X|x:
    echo 'You are leaving the Editing Menu'
  breaksw
  default:
    echo 'Enter D, E, F, or X'
  breaksw
endsw
```

If the user entered 1, D, or d in response to the menu prompt, the shell now executes the first branch (change directory). The shell prompts for a directory name, stores the name in $dir, and makes the change.

If the user entered 2, E, or e, the shell executes the second branch (edit a document); if the user entered 3, F, or f, the shell executes the third branch (format a document); if the user entered 4, X, or x, the shell executes the fourth branch (exit from this menu).

If the user entered any other number or letter, the fifth branch reprompts the user, repeating the valid choices. The **switch** statement always ends with **endsw**.

You must terminate each branch with **breaksw**. This statement enables you to use semicolons (;) within the branch, as illustrated in the example just shown.

Forming Loops

```
while (expression)          Loop while true
   command list
end
```

A simple example of a **while** loop follows:

```
set i=5
while ($i)
   echo 'Counter is $i'
   @ i--
end
```

The output of this loop is the following:

```
Counter is 5
Counter is 4
Counter is 3
Counter is 2
Counter is 1
```

The counter is initialized to 5. On the first iteration, it is displayed and decremented to 4. It is then decremented on each subsequent iteration until its value is 1. On the fifth iteration, the counter becomes zero and the loop ends.

```
label:                          Loop while false
   command list
goto label
```

A simple example of a loop follows:

```
@ set i = 1
start:
   @ i--
   echo Counter is $i
goto start
```

The output of this loop is the following:

```
Counter is 0
```

The counter is initialized to 1. On the first iteration, it is decremented to 0 and displayed. It is then decremented to -1 (a nonzero value) on the second iteration and the loop ends.

```
foreach variable (list)          Loop on variable
   command list
end
```

The **for** statement relies on a list of words, which can be either numbers or strings. Here is a simple example:

```
ingred='apple berry cake dough'
foreach word ($ingred)
   echo $word
end
```

The output of the preceding shell script is the following:

```
apple
berry
cake
dough
```

On each iteration, the shell selects another word from the list of words and displays it on the screen.

An alternate way to use the **for** statement is to generate a list from a UNIX command. Here is an example:

```
set 'ls'
foreach file
  echo $file
end
```

The output will be a list of the files in the current directory, generated by the **ls** command. When you use the **for** statement in this way, the **in** *list* statement becomes unnecessary. The following is equivalent to the previous shell script:

```
foreach file (*)
  echo $file
end
```

In the example, the asterisk (*) is replaced by the names of the files in the current directory.

The C shell enables you to assign all elements of an array to a variable in a single assignment. For example, fruit=(apple banana cherry) assigns three elements of an array to the variable fruit.

$var[sub]	The element of array *var* indicated by subscript *sub* (also ${sub[sub]})
$var[*]	All elements of array *var*
$var[i-j]	All elements of array *var* from element *i* through element *j* (also ${var[i-j]})
$var[$#sub]	The last element of array *var* (also ${sub[$#sub]})
$#var	Number of words in variable *var* (also $#{var})
$?var	One (1) if variable *var* is set; otherwise zero (0) (also $?{var})
$i	Positional parameter *i* (command line argument); use **$argv[$#var]** to obtain the last positional parameter

The following modifiers enable you to modify the values of variables. To clarify the explanations, let FILE=/usr/letter.txt.

:e	Return the suffix (the result of ${FILE:e} is txt)
:h	Return the first directory name (the result of ${FILE:h} is /usr)
:gh	Global h: apply globally to each element of an array
:q	Quote any words substituted, such as elements of an array; same as enclosing the name of the variable in double quotes (for example, ${LIST:q} is the same as "${LIST}")
:r	Remove the suffix (the result of ${FILE:r} is /usr/letter)
:gr	Global r: apply globally to each element of an array
:t	Return the basename (the result of ${FILE:t} is letter.txt)
:gt	Global t: apply globally to each element of an array
:x	Separate elements of an array (for example, ${LIST:x})

Defining a Function

You can assign any list of commands to a function name by using the format

```
name () { command list; }
```

For a function of any length, the format usually looks like this:

```
name ()
{
command list
}
```

Here is a simple example of a function:

```
rename ()
{
   echo "Current name: \c"
   set file=$<
   echo "Desired name: \c"
   set FILE=$<
   mv $file $FILE
   echo "File $file has been renamed $FILE \n"
}
```

This function renames a file with a short interactive dialog. Here is an example of using this function:

```
% rename
Current name: complicated
Desired name: simple
File complicated has been renamed simple
% _
```

The shell prompts you for the old name first, then the new name. Then it changes the name with the **mv** command. The shell function just described is very short and simple. For a real-life function that you use on your system, it would be desirable to incorporate safeguards into your function. For example, you would want to make sure that the target filename doesn't already exist.

Testing Files

The previous example of a function raised the issue of testing files. You can use any of the following expressions, enclosed within parentheses, in **if**, **foreach**, and **while** statements to check information about a file:

-e *file*	True if the file exists; otherwise, false
-z *file*	True if the size of the file is zero
-f *file*	True if the file is an ordinary file
-d *file*	True if the file is a directory
-r *file*	True if the file is readable
-w *file*	True if the file is writable
-x *file*	True if the file is executable

You could use one of these tests to enhance the **rename** function described earlier.

```
rename ()
{
   echo "Current name: \c"
   set file=$<
   echo "Desired name: \c"
   set FILE=$<
   if ( -f $FILE ) then
     echo "$FILE already exists"
   else
     mv $file $FILE
     echo "File $file has been renamed $FILE \n"
   endif
}
```

Comparing Variables

The shell enables you to perform any of six comparisons between two variables:

```
( $X == $Y )  Is X equal to Y?
( $X != $Y )  Is X not equal to Y?
```

```
( $X < $Y )    Is X less than Y?
( $X <= $Y )   Is X less than or equal to Y?
( $X > $Y )    Is X greater than Y?
( $X >= $Y )   Is X greater than or equal to Y?
```

For example, suppose **$min** is the minimum size you are looking for and **$size** is the size of the current file (called **$name**). You could test to determine whether the current file is the minimum size by using a script like the following:

```
min=20000
foreach name (*)
   size='wc -c < $name'
   if ( $size >= $min ) then
      echo "$name is a large file: $size characters"
   endif
end
```

The shell script just shown scans the current directory for large files (at least 20,000 characters long). Each time it finds one, it displays the name of the file and its length in characters. The **if** statement makes the actual comparison, testing the size of the current file against the minimum size.

Directory Substitution

Directory substitution, also known as tilde substitution, enables you to access commonly used directories more easily. The C shell supports the following notation:

~/dir   Subdirectory *dir* in your **$HOME** directory. For example, **cd ~/adm** would be equivalent to **cd /usr/jeff/adm**.

~name/dir   Subdirectory *dir* in the **$HOME** directory of user *name*. For example, **cd ~paul/test** would be equivalent to **cd/usr/paul/test**.

Command Substitution and Parameters

Command substitution means replacing a command with its output.

name=`command`

For example, you could use the following in a shell script:

```
list=`ls`
```

The effect of this command is to assign to variable **list** the names of the files in the current directory. If the directory contains five files called **art**, **cut**, **head**, **foot**, and **text**, the statement just shown is equivalent to the following:

```
list=(art cut head foot text)
```

Another way to use this kind of statement is as follows:

```
i=4
while ($i)
   @ i--
   echo $i
end
```

The initial value of the counter (i) is 4. The assignment that follows **while** reduces the value of i to 3 on the first iteration, then to 2, then to 1, then to 0, which ends the loop. The back quotes allow the **expr** statement to generate a new value for i. The value generated runs the loop through three iterations and also provides a mechanism for ending the loop.

The positional parameters represent the command and its arguments on the command line:

$0   The command itself
$1   The first argument
$2   The second argument
$3   The third argument (and so on up to 9)

For example, the **date** command generates five arguments:

```
% date
Thu Mar 25 15:08:19 1994
% _
```

In this example, $1 is Thu, $2 is Mar, $3 is 25, $4 is 15:08:19, and $5 is 1994. By using the **set** command, you can assign the positional parameters for subsequent use, as follows:

```
% set 'date'
% echo $5 \n
1994
% _
```

The **echo** command shown previously displays only the fifth argument of the **date** command, the year. You can also use positional parameters to rearrange the output of a command:

```
% echo 'Today is $1, $2 $3, $4 at $5 /n'
Today is Thu, Mar 25, 1994 at 15:08:19
% _
```

There are two ways to name a shell variable called *var*:

$*var*   Name variable *var*

${*var*}   Name variable *var*, with allowance for embedding into a
            string

For example, you could embed one string into another in the following
way:

```
% c=communica
% t=tele{$c}tions
% echo $t \n
telecommunications
% _
```

In this example, the shell embeds the string **c** (communica) into the
string **t**, which begins with tele and ends with tions. Without the braces,
this would have been impossible.

Reserved Shell Variables

The C shell sets these automatically. To obtain the current value of one of
these variables, precede its name with a dollar sign ($).

0   The name of the current shell script

?var   One (1) if *var* is set; otherwise, zero (0) (also {?*var*})

$ PID of the current process

<   Take one line of standard input

argv   Command line arguments for the current shell
               (positional parameters)

cwd   Current working directory

status   Status code of the most recent command

Built-In Shell Commands

You can use any of the following commands without starting a new
shell.

. *file*   Execute the commands in *file* as part of the current
                   process

break [*n*]   Exit from *n* levels of a **for** or **while** loop (by default,
                   one level)

continue [*n*]	Skip the rest of the current **for** or **while** loop and resume execution with the next iteration of the loop that is nested *n*-1 levels above the current loop (by default, the current loop)
cd [*directory*]	Change to *directory* indicated (by default **$HOME**)
echo *arg(s)*	Echo arguments (display on the screen)
eval [*arg(s)*]	Execute the arguments provided, allowing evaluation and substitution of shell variables
exec [*arg(s)*]	Execute the arguments provided without starting a new process
exit [*n*]	Exit from the current shell procedure with an exit value of *n*
export [*name(s)*]	Export the parameter(s) named to the environment of any commands subsequently executed; display exported variables

getopts *string var* [*arg(s)*] Check command options, using two mandatory arguments and one optional:

	string	List of valid option letters, followed by a colon (:) if the option has an argument of its own
	var	Variable into which to store the next option
	arg(s)	Check the arguments provided instead of the command line

hash [**-r**] [*name(s)*]	Set up a tracked alias for a command (same as **alias -t**), thereby speeding up execution; clear tracked aliases with the **-r** option
newgrp [**-**] [*group*]	Switch to *group*; if **-** is used, start with your login environment
pwd	Display the name of the current working directory
return [*n*]	Exit from a function with exit status *n* and return to the shell
set [*flag(s)*] [*arg(s)*]	Assign arguments *arg(s)* to the positional parameters; activate (-) or deactivate (+) *flag(s)* (from the following list) that affects the operation of the current shell; display the names and values of shell variables, along with the names and definitions of functions

	-/+a	Export/do not export variables that are created or modified
	-/+e	Exit/do not exit if a command exits with a nonzero (error) exit status

209

	-/+f	Disable/enable generation of filenames from wildcards
	-/+h	Hashing: Provide/do not provide quick access to commands used in a function
	-/+k	Keyword arguments: Provide/do not provide all keyword arguments (shell variables) for a command
	-/+n	Read but do not execute/execute commands
	-/+t	Execute/do not execute one command and exit
	-/+u	Cause/do not cause an error when attempting to substitute for an unset variable
	-/+v	Display/do not display input lines
	-/+x	Display/do not display command lines after they are ready for execution
shift [*n*]		Shift positional parameters *n* places (by default, one place) to the left
test		Test conditional expressions and set to true or false
times		Display cumulative user and system time for all processes run by the shell
trap [*cmd(s)*][*s*]		Trap signal number *s* and execute *cmd(s)*; if *s*=0, execute *cmd(s)* when the shell exits; if *cmd(s)* and *s* are omitted, display the commands currently being executed and the signal numbers currently being trapped
type [*name(s)*]		Display the full pathname of the command(s) named
ulimit [**-f** *b*]		Set a limit of *b* blocks for files created by the shell and its child processes; if the **-f** *b* option is omitted, display the current limit
umask [*mmm*]		Set the user creation mask *mmm*, which establishes permissions for new files created; if *mmm* is omitted, display the current user creation mask
unset [*name(s)*]		Unset the functions and variables named
wait [*n*]		Wait for process with PID *n* to complete in the background and display its exit status

D

The Korn Shell

Appendix D summarizes the command processor that was derived from the Bourne shell and the C shell, which is called the Korn shell. The Korn shell combines the efficiency of the Bourne shell with the enhancements of the C shell. Like the C shell, the Korn shell supports the history mechanism, arrays, command reentry, functions, and directory substitution.

```
$ ksh [option(s)] [argument(s)]
```

Options

-a	Mark modified export variables
-c *command*	Execute *command*; default is the first argument
-e	Exit if a command cannot be executed
-f	Disable wildcards
-i	Operate in interactive mode
-k	Place keywords in the environment
-m	Run background jobs in a separate process group
-n	Read only: Read commands but don't execute them
-o *arg(s)*	Set optional arguments (see **set** command)
-p	Do not process the **$HOME/.profile** file; replace the file designated in the ENV variable with the **/etc/suid_profile** file; do not set effective IDs to actual IDs (if the effective user ID (or group ID) is not equal to the actual user ID (or group ID), the **-p** option is set automatically)
-r	Restricted mode: Limit commands and directories
-s	Take commands from the standard input
-t	Execute one command and exit
-u	Cause an error when attempting to substitute an unset variable

| -v | Verbose: Display lines of input as they are being read |
| -x | Display command lines when executing them, preceded by a + |

Shell Variables

You can assign a shell variable on any command line, but you usually make assignments in your **.profile** file. Each assignment is of the form *variable=value* (for example, HOME=/usr/paul). Once a shell variable has been assigned, either explicitly or by default, you can invoke it by preceding its name with a dollar sign (for example, $HOME).

CDPATH	Search path for the **cd** command, with individual directory names separated by colons (:). Once CDPATH is set, you can give a relative pathname for a directory listed; then the shell will search the directories for the one intended. For example, with CDPATH=/usr/jeff/admin:/usr/jeff/ltrs:/usr/jeff/test set, you can refer to these directories as simply **admin**, **ltrs**, and **test**.
COLUMNS	Number of columns across your video screen (by default, 80), used by the **select** statement and the in-line editing mode.
EDITOR	Name of the default editor, typically **vi** or **emacs**.
ENV	Pathname of the environmental file, which contains aliases and functions. A typical name for the file is **.kshrc**.
FCEDIT	Name of the default editor for the **fc** command (by default, **/bin/ed**).
FPATH	Path list of directories that store functions, separated by colons; the **autoload** command uses this list.
HISTSIZE	The size of the history list, the number of prior commands that can be reexecuted.
HOME	Login directory; the **cd** command, without an argument, changes to this directory. For example, suppose you set HOME=/usr/jeff. Then, if you enter the **cd** command without an argument, the shell will

move you to **/usr/jeff**, which is often referred to as $HOME.

IFS Internal field separator (by default, spaces, tabs, and newlines). For example, suppose you set IFS=:. Then the shell will look for colons (instead of spaces, tabs, and newlines) to separate items on a line. The shell uses IFS to separate input fields used by **read**, positional parameters, and substituted commands.

LINES Number of lines used by the **select** statement for the select list.

LOGNAME Name of the user who owns the current shell.

MAIL Name of mail file. The shell will inform you whenever you receive mail in this file via the **mail** or **mailx** command. For example, suppose you set MAIL= /usr/jeff/admin/mail. Then, each time another user sends you mail, the shell will direct the mail to this file and inform you with the prompt **you have mail**. *See also* **MAILPATH** and **MAILCHECK**.

MAILCHECK Frequency with which the shell checks for mail (by default, 600 seconds, or every 10 minutes). If you set MAILCHECK=1800, the shell will check for mail every half hour. If you set MAILCHECK=0, the shell will check each time it displays its primary prompt on the screen.

MAILPATH Like **MAIL**, except that you can provide a list of mail files, each separated by a colon (:). For example, you could set MAILPATH=:/usr/jeff/admin/mail: /usr/jeff/test/mail. Then the shell will check both files, **/usr/jeff/admin/mail** and **/usr/jeff/test/mail**.

If you want to distinguish mail in one file from mail in another, you can assign to each a separate message. All you have to do is append to the filename a percent sign (%), followed by the message. For example, you could set MAILPATH=:/usr/jeff/admin/mail%you have administrative mail:/usr/jeff/test/mail%you have test mail. Then, if you receive mail in the first file, the shell prompt will be **you have administrative mail**; if you receive mail in the second file, the shell prompt will be **you have test mail**.

213

PATH　　　　　　Command file search path. The shell searches the
directories listed here for the names of any commands
you enter on the command line. For example, suppose
you set PATH=:/bin:/usr/bin:$HOME/bin. Then,
when you enter a command, the shell will search first
in **/bin**, then in **/usr/bin**, then in **$HOME/bin**. (If you
have already set HOME=/usr/jeff, the shell will
expand the variable and the third directory will be
/usr/jeff/bin.)

PS1　　　　　　Primary shell prompt (by default, $). As long as your
command lines each occupy a single line, the shell
displays only the dollar sign. *See also* **PS2**.

PS2　　　　　　Secondary shell prompt, used for commands that
cannot be completed on a single line (by default, >).
The appearance of this prompt indicates that the shell
expects more input before the end of the command
line. If a command line is too long to fit on a single
line, you can force an additional line (along with the
secondary shell prompt), by typing a backslash (\)
and pressing Enter. For example,

```
$ eqn /usr/pub/eqnchar letters | troff -cm | \
> col | lp
```

The shell will read these two lines as a single line of
input. (The backslash at the end of the line makes the
shell escape the newline generated when you press
Enter.)

PS3　　　　　　Tertiary shell prompt (by default, #?), used by the
select statement to obtain a response.

PS4　　　　　　Fourth-level shell prompt (by default, +), used during
a shell trace. It can be very handy to include
$LINENO in this prompt.

SHACCT　　　Shell accounting file, which is used to store
accounting records for all shell scripts executed. For
example, suppose you set SHACCT=/usr/jeff/adm/
shell. Then each time you execute a shell script, the
shell will append another accounting record to
/usr/jeff/adm/shell.

SHELL The shell to be used by commands when you escape to a subshell, of particular interest to **vi** and **ed**. The login shell also reads it to determine whether the user should be assigned a restricted shell. For example, you could set SHELL=/usr/lib/rksh to require a user to use the restricted shell.

The restricted shell prevents a user from redirecting output, using files outside the user's home directory, changing directories, or changing the command search path ($PATH).

TERM Terminal type, required by commands like **vi** that use the entire screen for output. For example, you could set TERM=vt100 to inform the shell that you are using a VT100 terminal.

TERMCAP Terminal capability directory (by default, **/etc/termcap**); superseded by TERMINFO but still used by some programs.

TERMINFO Terminal information directory (by default, **/usr/lib/terminfo**).

TMOUT Timeout value (the number of seconds without activity that will force an automatic logout). If TMOUT is not set or is set to zero, the timeout feature is disabled.

TZ Time zone used by the **date** command. For example, you could use **TZ=PST** for Pacific Standard Time.

VISUAL Same as EDITOR but takes precedence over EDITOR.

Input, Output, and Redirection

For each command executed, the shell opens three files, which are called the standard input, the standard output, and the standard error. By default, the standard input is the keyboard, and the standard output and standard error are the video screen. The shell assigns to each standard file a number called a *file descriptor*. The descriptor uses 0, 1, and 2 for standard input, standard output, and standard error; it uses higher numbers, starting at 3, for any other files required to complete the process. *Redirection* means directing output or input to or from a different file.

< *name*   Use *name* as the standard input. For example, with

```
$ mail jan < memo
```

you can mail the contents of **memo** to user jan.

> *name*   Use *name* as the standard output; if *name* doesn't already
exist, the shell creates it; if *name* does already exist, the
shell overwrites its contents. For example, with

```
$ sort list > list.sort
```

you can sort the contents of **list** and store the output in
list.sort.

>> *name*   Use *name* as the standard output, but append output to it
if it already exists. For example, with

$ sort list >> list.sort

you can sort the contents of **list** and append the output
to **list.sort**.

<< [-]*name*   Read input on secondary shell prompts until an input
line matches *name*, thereby producing a *here document*; if
the hyphen (-) is used, remove any initial tabs from input
lines. For example, with

```
$ cat - <<STOP
> Begin with this line
> This is the second line
> End with this line
> STOP
Begin with this line
This is the second line
End with this line
$ _
```

you can instruct the shell to continue accepting input
until the string that follows << appears as a line of input.
When that string appears, the document ends and the
command is carried out.

<&*d*   Use file descriptor *d* as the standard input

>&*d*   Use file descriptor *d* as the standard output, usually used
to save error messages (>&2)

<&-   Close the standard input

>&-   Close the standard output

Grouping and Connecting Commands

The shell offers a number of ways of grouping, listing, and connecting commands on a command line.

cmd1 | *cmd2*	Use the output of *cmd1* as the input for *cmd2*
cmd1; *cmd2*	Execute commands *cmd1* and *cmd2* consecutively; the semicolon acts as a newline
cmd &	Execute command *cmd* in the background
cmd |&	Shell pipe: execute command *cmd* in the background, with its input and output redirected through a two-way pipe. You can read from the pipe with the **read -p** command; you can write to it with the **print -p** command.
cmd1 && *cmd2*	AND: Execute command *cmd1*; if *cmd1* completes successfully, execute *cmd2*
cmd1 || *cmd2*	OR: Execute command *cmd1*; if *cmd1* does not complete successfully, execute *cmd2*
(*cmd1*; *cmd2*)	Create a subshell to execute commands *cmd1* and *cmd2*
{ *cmd1*; *cmd2*; }	Execute commands *cmd1* and *cmd2* using the current shell

Generating Filenames

Filenames can be generated from the following patterns:

?	Match any single character. For example, test.? can represent test.1, test.2, test.a, test.b, or test._.
*	Match any string of characters. For example, t*n can represent ten, tin, teen, tern, or turn.
[*list*]	Match any single character listed (the list can contain all the characters or show a range of characters). For example, [Bb]est can represent Best or best.
[!*list*]	Match any single character not listed. For example, t[!io]n can represent anything but tin or ton.

You can also combine these metacharacters in expressions. For example, [Tt]*n_? can represent Teen_a, turn_1, tan_0, or any of a number of other strings.

Quoting Characters

Removing the special meaning of a character like * is called *quoting* the character. To quote a single character, precede it with a backslash (\). For example, **t*t.*** can represent test.*, treat.*, or tart.*.

To quote an entire string, enclose the string between a pair of single quotes (' *string* ') or double quotes (" *string* "). Double quotes are similar to single quotes, except that double quotes do not quote the following metacharacters:

- `dollar sign ($)`
- `back quotes (' command ')`
- `backslash (\).`

Therefore, double quotes are better suited for expressions that contain shell variables (which begin with $) and command substitutions (which use ' and ').

Using the History File

You can set up automatic line numbering for your prompts by inserting an exclamation point (!). For example, if you place the line

```
set prompt="[!] "
```

in your **$HOME/.profile** file, it will display the following prompts when you begin work:

```
[1] _
[2] _
[3] _
...
```

Because the exclamation point has a special meaning in the Korn shell, you have to escape the exclamation point (\!) any time you use it for any purpose other than specifying an event.

Another line you can place in your **$HOME/.profile** file is one like the following:

```
HISTSIZE = 50
EXPORT $HISTSIZE
```

The effect of this line is to maintain a history file of the previous 50 events, or command lines that you have entered. You now can access any of these events for quick recall and reentry. To display a list of the events in your history file, enter the following command line:

```
[10] history
```

You can recall and execute events in your history file by using the following symbols. The Korn shell will first display the command line and then its output.

!!   Reinvoke the most recent event. For example:

```
[11] cat letter
. . .
[12] !!
cat letter
. . .
[13] _
```

!*n*   Reinvoke event number *n*. For example:

```
[13] !11
cat letter
. . .
[14] _
```

!-*i*   Reinvoke the event that is *i* lines prior to the current event. For example:

```
[14] !-3
cat letter
. . .
[15] _
```

!*x*   Reinvoke the most recent event that begins with character *x*. For example:

```
[15] !c
cat letter
. . .
[16] _
```

!?*x*   Reinvoke the event that contains character *x* anywhere on the line. For example:

```
[16] !?i
history
. . .
[17] _
```

With the following symbols, you can select individual arguments from an event in the history file. To illustrate, examine the following sample command line:

```
[17] echo arg1 arg2 arg3 arg4 arg5
arg1 arg2 arg3 arg4 arg5
[18] _
```

!*n*:*a* Select argument *a* from event *n*. For example:

```
[18] echo !!:3
echo arg3
arg3
[19] _
```

!*n*:*a-b* Select arguments *a-b* from event *n*. For example:

```
[19] echo 17:2-4
echo arg2 arg3 arg4
arg2 arg3 arg4
[20] _
```

!*n*:^ Select the first argument.

!*n*^ Select the first argument. For example:

```
[20] echo !17:^
echo arg1
arg1
[21] _
```

!*n*:$ Select the last argument.

!*n*$ Select the last argument. For example:

```
[21] echo !17:$
echo arg5
arg5
[22] _
```

!*n*:* Select all arguments.

!*n** Select all arguments. For example:

```
[22] echo !17:*
echo arg1 arg2 arg3 arg4 arg5
arg1 arg2 arg3 arg4 arg5
[23] _
```

With the three commands just shown, you can omit the colon (:).

You can use the following symbols to make substitutions in an event
before re-executing it:

!*n*:s/*word1*/*word2* Substitute: Replace *word1* with *word2* (first
occurrence only). For example:

```
[23] echo !17:s/a/A
echo Arg1 arg2 arg3 arg4 arg5
Arg1 arg2 arg3 arg4 arg5
[24] _
```

!*n*:*i*:s/*word1*/*word2*   Substitute: replace *word1* with *word2* (*i*th word only). For example:

```
[24] echo !17:5:s/a/A
echo Arg5
Arg5
[25] _
```

!*n*:gs/*word1*/*word2*   Global substitute: Replace *word1* with *word2* (every occurrence). For example:

```
[25] echo !17:gs/w/W
echo Arg1 Arg2 Arg3 Arg4 Arg5
Arg1 Arg2 Arg3 Arg4 Arg5
[26] _
```

!*n*:&   Repeat the previous substitution. For this example, return to command line 24:

```
[23] echo !17:s/a/A
echo Arg1 arg2 arg3 arg4 arg5
Arg1 arg2 arg3 arg4 arg5
[24] echo !!:&
echo Arg1 Arg2 arg3 arg4 arg5
Arg1 Arg2 arg3 arg4 arg5
[25] _
```

You can use the following symbols to modify a pathname in an event in the history file. To illustrate these, consider the following sample command line:

```
[30] echo /usr/jeff/adm/report.bak
/usr/jeff/adm/report.bak
[31] _
```

!*n*:h   Head: Remove the last name from a pathname. For example:

```
[31] echo !!:h
echo /usr/jeff/adm
/usr/jeff/adm
[32] _
```

!*n*:t   Tail: Remove the prefix from a pathname. For example:

```
[32] echo !30:t
echo report.bak
report.bak
[33] _
```

!*n*:r

Remove the suffix from a pathname. For example:

```
[33] echo !30:r
echo /usr/jeff/adm/report
/usr/jeff/adm/report
[34] _
```

You can use the following symbols to perform other functions on events in the history file:

!*n*:p

Print: Preview a command line without executing it. For example:

```
[34] echo !30:p
echo /usr/jeff/adm/report.bak
[35] _
```

!*n*:q

Quote: Protect a command line from further modification. For example:

```
[35] echo !30:q
echo /usr/jeff/adm/report.bak
/usr/jeff/adm/report.bak
[36] _
```

Using Aliases

The Korn shell supports *aliases*, which are substitute names for command lines. As with prompt and history information, you can store aliases in your **$HOME/.profile** file. You can set up a new alias with the **alias** command or remove an existing one with the **unalias** command. If you enter the **alias** command without an argument, it displays the aliases currently in effect, as shown here:

```
[40] alias
alias s1="vi /usr/jeff/pubs/section_1"
alias s2="vi /usr/jeff/pubs/section_2"
alias s3="vi /usr/jeff/pubs/section_3"
alias s4="vi /usr/jeff/pubs/section_4"
alias s5="vi /usr/jeff/pubs/section_5"
[41] _
```

The purpose of each alias is to enable you to enter a short command line like **s3** instead of a long command line like **vi /usr/jeff/pubs/section_3**.

You can allow for a dynamic selection by setting up the alias in the following way:

```
alias ss="vi /usr/jeff/pubs/section_\!*"
```

With this alias set up, either on a command line or in your **$HOME/.profile** file, you are now free to enter a command line like the following:

```
[41] ss 4
```

instead of

```
[41] vi /usr/jeff/pubs/section_4
```

You can combine several commands in a single alias, as long as you quote special symbols. Here is an example:

```
alias clp  'cd \!*; ls -l | page'
```

With this alias set up, either on a command line or in your **$HOME/.profile** file, you can now enter a command line like the following:

```
[42] clp ../ad
```

The effect of this command line is to execute the following command lines in succession:

```
cd ../adm
ls -l | page
```

The Korn shell first changes to the directory named, then displays a long listing of the files in that directory, piped to the **page** command to allow for easy viewing.

Finally, you can assign aliases recursively to as many levels as necessary. Here is an example:

```
[43] alias abc=def
[44] alias def=ghi
[45] alias ghi=clp
[46] abc /usr/jan/adm/tools
```

The effect of command line 46 is to invoke the alias **clp** with the argument **/usr/jan/adm/tools**.

Logical Constructions

The shell enables you to branch to another line of your shell program with the **if** and **case** statements. The Korn shell also enables you to construct loops with the **while, until,** and **for** statements.

Single Branching

```
if expression
    then command list
fi
```

For example, consider the following pair of shell scripts:

```
$ cat disp
if true
    then echo 'DISPLAY THIS'
fi
$ disp
DISPLAY THIS
$ _
```

The shell statement **true** forces the **then** statement to be executed. Therefore, the words are displayed on the screen.

```
$ cat trial
if false
    then echo 'DISPLAY THIS'
fi
$ trial
$ _
```

The Korn shell statement **false** prevents the **then** statement from being executed. Therefore, the text is not displayed.

```
if expression
    then command list 1
else command list 2
fi
```

For example, consider the following short shell script called **compare**:

```
$ cat compare
if c='expr "comparison" : "$1"'
    then echo " $c characters agree "
else echo 'No characters in common'
fi
$ _
```

To use this shell script, you have to enter its name followed by a string ($1). The shell compares the string you enter with the word comparison; then the shell assigns the number of consecutive characters matched to variable c. If any characters match, c is assigned a value equal to at least one (indicating true); if no characters match, c is assigned the value zero (indicating false). Here are two uses of **compare**:

```
$ compare compute
4 characters agree
$ _
```

In the first instance, the letters **comp** match and c is assigned the value 4, the number of matching letters. The shell substitutes 4 into the output. Because the value isn't zero, the expression is true and the shell executes the **then** statement.

```
$ compare zero
No characters in common
$ _
```

In the second instance, no characters match and c is assigned the value 0. Because the expression is false, the shell executes the **else** statement.

Multiple Branching

Branch to the command list that is prefaced by an expression that matches the *string*. The expressions *s1*, *s2*, *s3*, and so on, can be any alphanumeric combinations you choose. They can be single letters, numbers, or words. To allow more than one choice, you can separate the choices with OR symbols (|).

```
case string in
    s1) command list 1 ;;
    s2) command list 2 ;;
    s3) command list 3 ;;
    ...
    sn) command list n ;;
esac
```

The **case** statement often follows the selection of a choice. A user typically selects an item from a menu. The choice the user makes determines what the shell script does next. Here is an example:

```
echo '    EDITING MENU\n\n            '
echo '1  Change to directory      D or d'
echo '2  Edit                     E or e'
echo '3  Format                   F or f'
echo '4  Exit                     X or x'
echo '    Enter your selection: \c      '
read choice
```

The preceding lines will display the following on the screen:

```
   EDITING MENU
1  Change to directory          D or d
2  Edit                         E or e
3  Format                       F or f
4  Exit                         X or x
   Enter your selection: _
```

The menu displays four possible selections, with three ways of making each selection. For example, to change to a new directory, the user can enter 1, D, or d. The **read choice** statement at the end of the menu script above stores the user's response in a variable called **choice**. Now the **case** statement begins:

```
case $choice in
  1|D|d) echo 'Name of the new directory: \c'
         read dir; cd $dir ;;
  2|E|e) echo 'Name of document to edit: \c'
         read doc; vi $doc ;;
  3|F|f) echo 'Name of document to format: \c'
         read doc; ... ;;
  4|X|x) echo 'You are leaving the Editing Menu' ;;
  *)     echo 'Enter D, E, F, or X' ;;
esac
```

If the user entered 1, D, or d in response to the menu prompt, the shell now executes the first branch (change directory). The shell prompts for a directory name, stores the name in $dir, and makes the change.

If the user entered 2, E, or e, the shell executes the second branch (edit a document); if the user entered 3, F, or f, the shell executes the third branch (format a document); if the user entered 4, X, or x, the shell executes the fourth branch (exit from this menu).

If the user entered any other number or letter, the fifth branch reprompts the user, repeating the valid choices. The **case** statement always ends with **esac**, which is "case" spelled backward.

You must terminate each branch with a pair of semicolons (;;). This enables you to use single semicolons (;) within the branch, as illustrated in the example just shown.

Forming Loops

```
while command list 1          Loop while true
do command list 2
done
```

A simple example of a **while** loop follows:

```
i=5
while i='expr $i - 1'
do echo Counter is $i
done
```

The output of this loop is the following:

```
Counter is 4
Counter is 3
Counter is 2
Counter is 1
```

The counter is initialized to 5. On the first iteration, it is decremented to 4 and displayed. It is then decremented on each subsequent iteration until its value is 1. On the fifth iteration, the counter becomes zero and the loop ends.

```
until command list 1          Loop while false
do command list 2
done
```

A simple example of an **until** loop follows:

```
i=1
until i='expr $i - 1'
do echo Counter is $i
done
```

The output of this loop will be the following:

```
Counter is 0
```

The counter is initialized to 1. On the first iteration, it is decremented to 0 and displayed. It is then decremented to -1 (a nonzero value) on the second iteration and the loop ends.

```
for variable in list          Loop on variable
   do command list
done
```

The **for** statement relies on a list of words, which can be either numbers or strings. Here is a simple example:

```
ingred='apple berry cake dough'
for word in $ingred
   do echo $word
done
```

The output of the shell script just shown is the following:

```
apple
berry
cake
dough
```

On each iteration, the shell selects another word from the list of words and displays it on the screen.

An alternate way to use the **for** statement is to generate a list from a UNIX command. Here is an example:

```
set 'ls'
for file
   do echo $file
done
```

The output will be a list of the files in the current directory, generated by the **ls** command. When you use the **for** statement in this way, the **in** *list* statement becomes unnecessary. The following is equivalent to the previous shell script:

```
for file in *
   do echo $file
done
```

In the example, the asterisk (*) is replaced by the names of the files in the current directory.

Defining a Function

You can assign any list of commands to a function name by using the format

```
name () { command list; }
```

For a function of any length, the format usually looks like this:

```
name ()
{
command list
}
```

Here is a simple example of a function:

```
rename ()
{
echo "Current name: \c"
read file
echo "Desired name: \c"
read FILE
mv $file $FILE
echo "File $file has been renamed $FILE \n"
}
```

This function renames a file with a short interactive dialog. Here is an example of using this function:

```
$ rename
Current name: complicated
Desired name: simple
File complicated has been renamed simple
$ _
```

The shell prompts you for the old name first, then the new name. Then it changes the name with the **mv** command. The shell script just described is very short and simple. For a real-life script that you use on your system, it would be desirable to incorporate safeguards into your script. For example, you would want to make sure that the target filename doesn't already exist.

Testing Files

The previous example of a function raised the issue of testing files. The shell offers you five different tests:

[-r name]	File *name* exists and can be read
[-w name]	File *name* exists and can be written to
[-f name]	File *name* exists and is not a directory
[-d name]	File *name* exists and is a directory
[-s name]	File *name* exists and is not empty

You could use one of these tests to enhance the **rename** function described earlier.

```
rename ()
{
echo "Current name: \c"
read file
echo "Desired name: \c"
read FILE
```

```
if [ -f $FILE ]
   then echo "$FILE already exists"
   else mv $file $FILE
   echo "File $file has been renamed $FILE \n"
fi
}
```

Comparing Quantities

The shell enables you to perform any of six comparisons between two numerical quantities:

```
[ X -eq Y ]    Is X equal to Y?
[ X -ne Y ]    Is X not equal to Y?
[ X -lt Y ]    Is X less than Y?
[ X -le Y ]    Is X less than or equal to Y?
[ X -gt Y ]    Is X greater than Y?
[ X -ge Y ]    Is X greater than or equal to Y?
```

For example, suppose **$min** is the minimum size you are looking for and **$size** is the size of the current file (called **$name**), then you could test to determine whether the current file is the minimum size by using a script like the following:

```
min=20000
for name in *
   do size='wc -c < $name'
   if [ $size -ge $min ]
      then echo "$name is a large file: $size characters"
   fi
done
```

The shell script just shown scans the current directory for large files (at least 20,000 characters long). Each time it finds one, it displays the name of the file and its length in characters. The **if** statement makes the actual comparison, testing the size of the current file against the minimum size.

Comparing Strings

The shell can test strings also, using one of four different tests:

```
[ -n string ]    Does the string exist?
[ -z string ]    Does the string not exist?
[ s1 = s2 ]      Are the two strings the same?
[ s1 != s2 ]     Are the two strings not the same?
```

In the second test shown, -z is equivalent to !-n. In the first test shown, you can omit -n. You can test for the existence of a string in one of two ways:

```
if [ -n "$1" ]
```

or

```
if [ "$1" ]
```

You can also test for the nonexistence of a string in one of two ways:

```
if [ !-n "$1" ]
```

or

```
if [ -z "$1" ]
```

The double quotes are used in these examples to retain the meanings of special characters and treat spaces as characters. If you want the shell to disregard spaces, you can omit the double quotes, as shown:

```
if [ $first = $third ]
```

This example will be true if the two variables are identical or even if they are the same except for spaces. For example, they could be assigned the following values and still be identical:

```
first='  train'
third=train
```

As shown, the equal sign used in an assignment statement can be entered without surrounding spaces. However, when an equal sign (or a not equal sign) is used in a comparison, it must be surrounded by spaces. For example, you must enter

```
if [ $first = $third ]
```

not

```
if [ $first=$third ]          [not acceptable]
```

Compound Testing

To perform compound testing of files, quantities, or strings, you can use the following logical operators:

-a AND: True only if both statements are true
-o OR: True if either statement is true
! NOT: True becomes false; false becomes true

For example,

```
if [ ! false ]
```

is equivalent to

```
if [ true ]
```

The statement

```
if [ -f $name -a -r $name -o -w $name ]
```

checks to determine whether a file called name exists and is either readable or writable by the owner of the script.

Directory Substitution

Directory substitution, also known as tilde substitution, enables you to access commonly used directories more easily. The Korn shell supports the following notation:

~/*dir*	Subdirectory *dir* in your **$HOME** directory. For example, **cd ~/adm** would be equivalent to **cd /usr/jeff/adm**.
~*name*/*dir*	Subdirectory *dir* in the **$HOME** directory of user *name*. For example, **cd ~paul/test** would be equivalent to **cd /usr/paul/test**.
~-	Your previous working directory
~+	Full pathname of your current directory

Command Substitution and Parameters

Command substitution means replacing a command with its output.

```
name='command'
```

For example, you could use the following in a shell script:

```
list='ls'
```

The effect of this command is to assign to variable **list** the names of the files in the current directory. If the directory contains five files called **art**, **cut**, **head**, **foot**, and **text**, the statement just shown is equivalent to the following:

```
list='art cut head foot text'
```

Another way to use this kind of statement is as follows:

```
i=4
while i='expr $i - 1'
  do echo $i
done
```

The initial value of the counter (i) is 4. The assignment that follows **while** reduces the value of i to 3 on the first iteration, then to 2, then to 1, then to 0, which ends the loop. The back quotes allow the **expr** statement to generate a new value for i. The value generated runs the loop through three iterations and also provides a mechanism for ending the loop.

The positional parameters represent the command and its arguments on the command line:

$0 The command itself
$1 The first argument
$2 The second argument
$3 The third argument (and so on, up to 9)

For example, the **date** command generates five arguments:

```
$ date
Thu Mar 25 15:08:19 1994
$ _
```

In this example, $1 is Thu, $2 is Mar, $3 is 25, $4 is 15:08:19, and $5 is 1994. By using the **set** command, you can assign the positional parameters for subsequent use, as follows:

```
$ set `date`
$ echo $5 \n
1994
$ _
```

The **echo** command shown previously displays only the fifth argument of the **date** command, the year. You can also use positional parameters to rearrange the output of a command:

```
$ echo 'Today is $1, $2 $3, $4 at $5 /n'
Today is Thu, Mar 25, 1994 at 15:08:19
$ _
```

There are two ways to name a shell variable called *var*:

$var   Name variable *var*
${var} Name variable *var*, with allowance for embedding into a string

For example, you could embed one string into another in the following way:

```
$ c=communica
$ t=tele{$c}tions
$ echo $t \n
telecommunications
$ _
```

In this example, the shell embeds the string **c** (communica) into the string **t**, which begins with tele and ends with tions. Without the braces, this would have been impossible.

You can refer to arrays and elements in arrays using the following notation:

$var[sub]   The value of the element of array *var*, subscript *sub*

${var[sub]}   The value of the element of array *var*, subscript *sub* (same as previous item)

${var[*]}   All values of all elements of array *var*

${#var}   The number of characters used in the value of the variable; if *var=**, display the positional parameters

${#var[*]}   The number of elements in array *var*

Conditional substitution enables you to make assignments depending on prior assignment of values.

${var:-string} If *var* has been assigned a value that is not null, the value of this expression is $var; otherwise, it is $string

${var-string}   If *var* has been assigned a value (even if it is null), the value of this expression is $var; otherwise, it is $string

Here is an example, with one variable assigned and one left unassigned:

```
$ fruit=pear
$ veg=
$ echo ${fruit:-apple} with ${veg:-carrot}
pear with carrot
$ _
```

As another example, suppose you want to make a backup copy of a file. Suppose further that you want to have the option of naming a particular target directory. It is understood that if you don't name the directory, the backup copy will be placed in the current directory. Then you could use something like the following in a shell script called **backup**:

```
file=$1
dir=${2:-.}
cp $file $dir/{$file}_bak
```

As this partial shell script indicates, you must name the file to be backed up as the first argument ($1), but you don't necessarily have to name the target directory as the second argument ($2). So you can enter **backup** in one of two ways:

```
$ backup test
```

This command line makes a backup copy of **test**, called **test_bak**, in the current directory.

```
$ backup test $HOME/archive
```

This second command line makes a backup copy of **test**, called **test_bak**, in a subdirectory of your login directory called **archive**.

${*var*:=*string*}   If *var* has been assigned a value that is not null, the value of this expression is $*var*; otherwise, it is $*string*; in addition, the shell assigns the value of *string* to *var*

${*var*=*string*}   If *var* has been assigned a value (even if it is null), the value of this expression is $*var*; otherwise, it is $*string*; in addition, the shell assigns the value of *string* to *var*

To reuse the example introduced earlier, you could use the following lines:

```
file=$1
dir=$2
echo Target directory is ${dir:='pwd'}
cp $file $dir/{$file}_bak
```

If the name of the target directory is entered on the command line as the second argument ($2), then that is the name used. If no name is entered, the shell assigns the name of the current directory and that is the name used.

${*var*:+*string*}   If *var* has been assigned a value that is not null, the value of this expression is $*string*; otherwise, it is null and the value of *var* remains unassigned

${*var*+*string*}   If *var* has been assigned a value (even if it is null), the value of this expression is $*string*; otherwise, it is null and the value of *var* remains unassigned

For example, suppose you have a variable called MSG that determines whether to display a message on the screen. If MSG is unassigned, there is no message; if MSG is assigned, there is a message, but it will be the message shown here. In this way, one variable can control what happens on many different lines of your shell script.

```
echo ${MSG:+'Incorrect specification
entered\n'}
```

If MSG has been assigned a value, the shell displays the message **Incorrect specification entered** here; if MSG has not been assigned a value, no message appears here.

${*var*:?*string*} If *var* has been assigned a value that is not null, the value of this expression is $*var*; otherwise, display *string* and exit; if *string* is empty, display a default message and exit

${*var*?*string*} If *var* has been assigned a value (even if it is null), the value of this expression is $*var*; otherwise, display a message and exit

For example, consider the following lines:

```
$ OK='No problem here'
$ echo ${OK:nok} \n
No problem here
$ _
```

Because the variable OK has an assigned value, that value is displayed and processing continues.

But suppose variable OK is unassigned, as shown here:

```
$ nok='Variable not set -- abort'
$ echo ${OK:nok} \n
test: OK: Variable not set -- abort
$ _
```

Because variable OK has no assigned value, the shell displays the value of variable nok and aborts immediately.

${*var*## *string*} The value of *var* with the longest matching pattern in *string* removed from the left side; if there is no match, use the value of *var* intact; pattern *string* may contain wildcard characters

${*var#string*}   The value of *var* with the shortest matching pattern in *string* removed from the left side; if there is no match, use the value of *var* intact; pattern *string* may contain wildcard characters

${*var%%string*} The value of *var* with the longest matching pattern in *string* removed from the right side; if there is no match, use the value of *var* intact; pattern *string* may contain wildcard characters

${*var%string*}   The value of *var* with the shortest matching pattern in *string* removed from the right side; if there is no match, use the value of *var* intact; pattern *string* may contain wildcard characters

Reserved Shell Variables

The following shell variables provide system information:

$0   Name of the current shell script

$#   Number of arguments in a command line

For example, suppose we check the **date** command again:

```
$ set 'date'
$ echo $# \n
5
$ _
```

The shell responds by displaying 5, the number of arguments output by the **date** command.

$?   Exit code of the command most recently executed in the foreground:

```
$ date
Thu Mar 25 15:08:19 1994
$ echo $? \n
0
$ _
```

The return code is zero, meaning the process was executed successfully. A nonzero return code means an error in execution.

$$ PID of the current shell script

Because the process ID of each process is unique, it is sometimes used in the name of a temporary file. Here is an example:

```
$ tmp=sort$$
$ sort table -o $tmp
$ mv $tmp table
$ _
```

In this example, we needed a place to store the output of the **sort** command. The name chosen was **sort**, followed by the process ID of the **sort** command.

$!   PID of the most recent background process

You can use this variable to recall the process ID, as shown here:

```
$ echo $! \n
1073
$ _
```

With the number recalled, you can kill the process if necessary.

$-   Hyphen: Shell options currently in effect

You can use this variable to display which flags are currently set, as shown here:

```
$ echo $- \n
e
$ _
```

Only the e (exit) flag is set. See the **set** command later in this appendix.

$*   All positional parameters for the current shell script (as a single argument)

$@   All positional parameters for the current shell script (as separate arguments)

$_   Underline: The last argument of the most recent command. For example, after entering **mm art book center**, you can enter **cat $_** to display file **center**.

$ERRNO   Error number of the most recent system call, listed in **/usr/include/sys/errno.h**

$LINENO   Current line number of the current shell script

$OLDPWD   Directory before the most recent **cd** command

$OPTARG   The option argument that follows an argument for the **getopts** command

$OPTIND   Index of the option that the **getopts** command will process next

$PPID   Process ID of the parent

$PWD   Current working directory

$RANDOM Random number, updated each time it is referred to

$REPLY   Used by the **keyword** statement and by others if there is no variable

$SECONDS Time in seconds since you started the current shell

Built-In Shell Commands

You can use any of the following commands without starting a new shell.

:	Null command: The shell performs no action and returns an execution code of zero
. *file*	Execute the commands in *file* as part of the current process
break [*n*]	Exit from *n* levels of a **for** or **while** loop (by default, one level)
continue [*n*]	Skip the rest of the current **for** or **while** loop and resume execution with the next iteration of the loop that is nested *n*-1 levels above the current loop (by default, the current loop)
cd [*directory*]	Change to *directory* indicated (by default **$HOME**)
echo *arg(s)*	Echo arguments (display on the screen)
eval [*arg(s)*]	Execute the arguments provided, allowing evaluation and substitution of shell variables
exec [*arg(s)*]	Execute the arguments provided without starting a new process
exit [*n*]	Exit from the current shell procedure with an exit value of *n*
export [*name(s)*]	Export the parameter(s) named to the environment of any commands subsequently executed; show exported variables

239

getopts *string var* [*arg(s)*] Check command options, using two mandatory arguments and one optional:

    string   List of valid option letters, followed by a colon (:) if the option has an argument of its own

    var   Variable into which to store the next option

    arg(s)   Check the arguments provided instead of the command line

hash [-r] [*name(s)*] Set up a tracked alias for a command (same as **alias -t**), thereby speeding up execution; clear tracked aliases with the **-r** option

newgrp [-] [*group*] Switch to *group*; if - is used, start with your login environment

pwd Display the name of the current working directory

read [*name(s)*] Read from the standard input and assign input to the name(s) provided

readonly [*name(s)*] Make the variables named read-only, thereby prohibiting further assignment

set [*flag(s)* [*arg(s)*] Assign arguments *arg(s)* to the positional parameters; activate (-) or deactivate (+) *flag(s)* (listed here) that affects the operation of the current shell; display the names and values of shell variables, along with the names and definitions of functions

    -/+a   Export/do not export variables that are created or modified

    -/+e   Exit/do not exit if a command exits with a nonzero (error) exit status

    -/+f   Disable/enable generation of filenames from wildcards

    -/+h   Hashing: Provide/do not provide quick access to commands used in a function

	-/+k	Keyword arguments: Provide/do not provide all keyword arguments (shell variables) for a command
	-/+n	Read but do not execute/execute commands
	-/+t	Execute/do not execute one command and exit
	-/+u	Cause/do not cause an error when attempting to substitute for an unset variable
	-/+v	Display/do not display input lines
	-/+x	Display/do not display command lines after they are ready for execution
shift [*n*]		Shift positional parameters *n* places (by default, one place) to the left
test		Test conditional expressions and set to true or false; use either the **test** command or a pair of brackets
times		Display cumulative user and system time for all processes run by the shell
trap [*cmd(s)*][*s*]		Trap signal number *s* and execute *cmd(s)*; if *s*=0, execute *cmd(s)* when the shell exits; if *cmd(s)* and *s* are omitted, display the commands currently being executed and the signal numbers currently being trapped
type [*name(s)*]		Display the full pathname of the command(s) named
ulimit [**-f** *b*]		Set a limit of *b* blocks for files created by the shell and its child processes; if the **-f** *b* option is omitted, display the current limit
umask [*mmm*]		Set the user creation mask *mmm*, which establishes permissions for new files created; if *mmm* is omitted, display the current user creation mask

unset [*name(s)*]   Unset the functions and variables named

wait [*n*]   Wait for process with PID *n* to complete in the background and display its exit status

E

The awk/nawk Programming Language

Appendix E provides a description of the **awk** programming language, along with the enhanced **nawk** (new **awk**) programming language. This language, which is most suitable for files that contain tabular material, enables you to search for text in a file and then take some predetermined action when it finds the text in a line.

The program for an **awk** (or **nawk**) command line specifies a pattern to be matched, followed by an action statement (or a series of statements), enclosed between braces. You can either enter the program right on the command line, enclosing its name between a pair of single quotes, or enter the program into a separate file, which you can call from the command line. A separate file is best suited for longer programs that require many lines.

```
$ nawk [-Fx] 'program' [var=value] [file(s)] [-]
$ nawk [-Fx] -f file [var=value] [file(s)] [-]
```

Options and Arguments

-Fx	Field separator: separate fields with character x (by default, spaces and tabs)
'program'	You can enter the program directly on the command line, using the format ' *pattern* { *action* } '
-f *file*	Another approach is to enter the program into *file* (without single quotes) and then use the -f option to call the file
var=value	You can assign values to variables on the command line if necessary
file(s)	You can name a file (or a series of files) to be scanned
-	You can also take input from the keyboard, which can be intermingled with files

You can omit either the *pattern* or the *action* statement in a program, but not both. If you omit the *pattern*, **awk** selects all lines of input; if you omit the *action*, **awk** displays all lines unmodified.

Records and Fields

It is understood that **awk** processes files that contain tabular material. Each line in the file represents one *record*; each line contains a set of columns called *fields*. The first field is denoted $1; the second field, $2; the third, $3; and so on. The notation for an entire record is $0.

Patterns

The *pattern* is what **awk** uses to select lines of input. The *action* is carried out only on those lines matched by the *pattern*. The default *pattern* is all input lines.

Patterns usually contain *regular expressions*, which are as follows:

.	Match any single character
[*list*]	Match any character listed (for example, [abc])
[!*list*]	Do not match any character listed (for example, [!abc])
[*x-y*]	Match any character in the range indicated (for example, [a-c])
expr1 | *expr2*	Match either of the expressions shown (for example, [a-c] | [x-z])
expr?	Match zero or one occurrence of *expr*
*expr**	Match zero or more occurrences of *expr*
expr+	Match one or more occurrences of *expr*
^	Match the beginning of the line
$	Match the end of the line
\	Escape the special meaning of a metacharacter

The escape character (\) is used to match various control characters in the following *escape characters*:

\b	Match a backspace

\f	Match a formfeed
\n	Match a newline
\r	Match a carriage return
\t	Match a tab
\0*ccc*	Match ASCII code 0*ccc*
x	Match literal character *x* ˙

You can combine regular expressions with a number of operators:

/*expr*/	Match if the input line contains *expr*. For example, **nawk '/ox/' animals** (which is equivalent to **nawk '$0 ~ /ox/' animals**) will match every line in file **animals** that contains **ox**.
string ~ *expr*	Match if *string* contains *expr*. For example, **nawk ' $3 ~ /[Tt]iger/ ' animals** will match every line in file animals in which the third field contains either **Tiger** or **tiger**.
string !~ *expr*	Match if *string* note *expr*. For example, **nawk ' $4 !~ /[Aa]ntelope/ ' animals** will match every line in file **animals** in which the fourth field does not contain either **Antelope** or **antelope**.
v1 == *v2*	Match if *v1* is equal to *v2*. For example, **nawk ' $2 == "Wolf" ' animals** will match every line in file **animals** in which the second field equals **Wolf**.
v1 != *v2*	Match if *v1* is not equal to *v2*. For example, **nawk ' $2 != "Wolf" ' animals** will match every line in file **animals** in which the second field equals anything but **Wolf**.
v1 < *v2*	Match if *v1* is less than *v2*. For example, **nawk ' $5 < "100" ' animals** will match every line in file **animals** in which the fifth field is less than 100.
v1 <= *v2*	Match if *v1* is less than or equal to *v2*. For example, **nawk ' $2 <= "C" ' animals** will match every line in file **animals** in which the second field begins with A, B, or C.
v1 > *v2*	Match if *v1* is greater than *v2*. For example, **nawk ' $5 > "200" ' animals** will match every line in file **animals** in which the fifth field is greater than 200.

v1 >= *v2*   Match if *v1* is greater than or equal to *v2*. For example, **nawk ' $2 >= "W" '** **animals** will match every line in file **animals** in which the second field begins with W, X, Y, or Z.

By using the following operators, you can form compound statements:

&&   AND: Match if both expressions match. For example, **nawk ' $6 < "c" && $6 != "bat" '** **animals** will match every line in file **animals** in which the sixth field begins with a or b, but doesn't contain **bat**.

| | OR: Match if either expression matches. For example, **nawk ' $2 == "deer" | | $5 == "150" '** **animals** will match every line in file **animals** in which either the second field contains **deer** or the fifth field contains **150**.

( )   Grouping: Match expressions as a unit. For example, **nawk ' ($5 == "100" | | $5 == "200") && $2 == "deer" '** **animals** will match every line in file **animals** in which the fifth field contains either 100 or 200 and the second field contains **deer**.

!   Negation: Match if the expression does not match. For example, **nawk ' ! /deer/ '** **animals** will match every line in file **animals** that does not contain **deer**.

,   Range: Match a range of values. For example, **nawk ' /coyote/,/fox/ '** **animals** will match every line in file **animals** that contains any name between, and including, **coyote** and **fox**.

Two patterns deserve special mention. Neither pattern matches text; both are used to handle processing before and after pattern-matching.

BEGIN   This pattern enables you to carry out initialization actions before pattern-matching begins.

END   This pattern enables you to carry out finalization actions after completion of pattern-matching.

A typical **nawk** program may include three sections:

* Preliminary actions, such as displaying a header message or setting variables, preceded by **BEGIN**
* Pattern-matching actions (the main program)
* Concluding actions, such as computing totals or averages, preceded by **END**

Actions

The action, which must be enclosed between a pair of braces, is performed only if the pattern preceding it is matched. The default action is { **print** }, or { **print $0** }, which causes the entire record to be sent to the output.

The action may include constants, variables, arrays, conditional statements, loops, arithmetic operations, mathematical functions, string operations, control statements, and sophisticated output.

If you want to document your code, you can use a number sign (#) to begin comments on any line of an **awk/nawk** program.

You can use any of the following built-in variables in an **awk/nawk** program:

ARGC	The number of arguments on a command line
ARGV	The name of the array that contains the arguments.
ENVIRON	Environment passed from the shell to **awk/nawk**
FILENAME	Name of the current input file
FNR	Number of the current record
FS	Field separator (by default, spaces and tabs)
NF	Number of the current field
NR	Number of records processed
OFMT	Output format for numbers processed by the **printf** command (by default, %.6g)
ORS	Output record separator (by default, newline)
RLENGTH	Length of a string that the **match** function matches
RSTART	The starting position of any string that the **match** function matches
RS	Input record separator (by default, newline)
SUBSEP	The subscript separator (by default, ^\)

As indicated earlier, fields are identified by number. The first field is $1, the second is $2, the third is $3, and so on. You can also name fields in a loop using a variable (for example, $i). For example, to send every even-numbered record to the output, you could use a statement like the following, which is modeled after the C language:

```
for ( i = 2; i <= NF; i+=2 )
   print $i
```

As illustrated in this example, you are free to assign and use any variables you need to complete your program. In the example just shown, **i** is used as a counter to step through the records. With **awk/nawk**, no prior declaration or initialization is necessary. Furthermore, you can convert the variable type freely between string and floating-point numeric at any point in your program. Here are a few examples:

a = 8	Assign 8 to **x**, thereby making x floating point
b = "bar"	Assign **bar** to **b**, thereby making **b** a string variable
c = "3" + "2"	Assign **5** (the sum of 3 and 2) to **c**, thereby making c floating point
b = "bar" + 0	Add zero to **b**, thereby converting **b** to floating point
a = 8""	Concatenate a null string to the current value of **a**, thereby converting **a** to a string variable

An *array* is a set of variables that share a common name. Each individual element in the array is *indexed* for subsequent reference. Like user-defined variables, arrays in an **awk/nawk** program require neither declaration nor initialization. The indexes for your arrays can be either numeric or string variables; they can also be built-in variables. Here is a simple example of an array:

```
CITY[1] = "San Diego"
CITY[2] = "Los Angeles"
CITY[3] = "San Jose"
CITY[4] = "San Francisco"
CITY[5] = "Sacramento"
```

In this example, the name of the array is **CITY**, whereas the individual elements are names of major cities in California. Each element, or city name, has its own index (in this instance a number). The index for San Diego is 1, the index for Los Angeles is 2, and so on. If you had the array just shown set up and assigned, you could use a statement like the following to send the name of each city to the output:

```
for ( i = 1; i <= NR; i++ )
  print CITY[i]
```

Suppose a file called **cities** contains the following information:

```
San Diego       619     92101*      697,027     816,659
Los Angeles     213*    90001*      2,811,801   2,787,176
San Jose        408     95101*      459,913     592,773
San Francisco   415     94101*      715,674     649,315
Sacramento      916     95801*      257,105     274,488
```

where the various columns contain (1) the name of the city, (2) the area code (* indicates more than one), (3) the zip code (* indicates more than one), (4) the population in 1970, and (5) the population in 1980.

Then suppose a file called **check** contains the following program:

```
BEGIN   { print "Population of Cities in 1980"
        print "City            Population" }
        { city[NR] = $1; pop80[NR] = $5 }
END     { for ( i = 1; i <= NR; i++ )
        print city[i] price[i] }
```

Then you could process file **cities** with the program in file **check** in the following way:

```
$ nawk -f check cities
Population of Cities in 1980
City            Population
San Diego       816,659
Los Angeles     2,787,176
San Jose        592,773
San Francisco   649,315
Sacramento      274,488
$ _
```

In this example, the **nawk** program is in three sections: the BEGIN section (two lines), the main section (one line), and the END section (two lines).

The BEGIN section places two lines of a heading at the top. The main section assigns city names to an array called **city** and populations in 1980 to an array called **pop80**. In each instance, the built-in variable NR (the number of the current record) is used as the index. The END section sets up a loop that steps through the two arrays while displaying their elements.

Note that in the main section NR is a variable that increases by one with each new record processed; whereas in the END section NR has become, in effect, a constant (the total number of records, 5).

When writing an **awk/nawk** program, you can use a number of built-in functions for strings and numbers. The string functions are as follows:

delete *array[element]*	Delete an element from an array
gsub(*old,new*)	Globally substitute *new* for *old* in the current record and return the number of substitutions made
gsub(*old,new,string*)	Globally substitute *new* for *old* in *string* and return the number of substitutions made

index(*STRING,string*)	Return the position in *STRING* where *string* begins (or 0 if *string* isn't found)
length(*string*)	Return the number of characters in *string*
match(*STRING,string*)	Search *STRING* for a match for *string*, and return the starting position (or 0 if *string* isn't found)
split(*string,array*[,*fs*])	Split *string* into elements of *array*, using either the optional field separator *fs* or, in the absence of *fs*, the value of the variable FS
sprintf(*format,expr1,expr2,...*)	Return the expressions indicated, using **printf** formatting statement *format*
sub(*old,new*)	Search the current record for *old* and replace with *new*
sub(*old,new,string*)	Search *string* for *old* and replace with *new*
substr(*string,pos*[,*len*])	Return the substring of *string* that begins at position *pos* and has length *len*

The numeric functions are as follows:

cos(*x*)	Return the cosine of *x* (*x* in radians)
exp(*x*)	Return the value of **e** (Euler's number) to the power *x*
int(*x*)	Truncate *x* to its integer value
log(*x*)	Return the natural logarithm of *x* (base **e**)
rand(!)	Return a random number between zero and one
sin(*x*)	Return the sine of *x* (*x* in radians)
sqrt(*x*)	Return the square root of *x*
srand(*x*)	Make *x* the seed for the random number function

You can also define your own functions. All you have to do is use the following format:

```
name(par1,par2,par3,...) {
   statement(s)
}
```

For example, you could define a function called fill that assigns values to

```
file (i,n) {
   for ( i = 1; i<= NR; i++ )
```

```
value[NR] = $4 + $5
}
```

The arithmetic operators, which are borrowed from the C language, are as follows:

+   Add
-     Subtract
*   Multiply
/   Divide
%   Take remainder (modulus)

The assignment operators that you can use with variables are as follows:

++   Increment (**i++** is equivalent to **i = i + 1**)
+=   Add and assign (**i+=p** is equivalent to **i = i + p**)
--   Decrement (**i--** is equivalent to **i = i - 1**)
-=   Subtract and assign (**i-=p** is equivalent to **i = i - p**)
*=   Multiply and assign (**i*=p** is equivalent to **i = i * p**)
/=   Divide and assign (**i/=p** is equivalent to **i = i / p**)
%=   Take remainder (modulus) and assign (**i%=p** is equivalent to **i = i % p**)

You can also use the following relational operators to make comparisons:

a < b   a is less than b
a > b   a is greater than b
a <= b   a is less than or equal to b
a >= b   a is greater than or equal to b
a == b   a is equal to b
a != b   a is not equal to b

Variables that you use as arguments cannot be changed within the function and returned to the main program. However, variables not listed as arguments can be changed within the function and returned to the main program. On the other hand, arrays can always be altered within a function and returned.

The most common mode of reading input for **awk/nawk** is to read from a file. Here is a simple example, which sends to the output every line that contains the word *system*:

```
$ nawk ' /system/ ' report
each system must include the proper controls for
to which the newest systems must conform for maximum
```

```
data entry. The system must then process the entire
$ _
```

However, you can also read input from the keyboard or through a pipe. Here is an example of reading input that is passed from another program to **nawk** via a pipe:

```
$ cat /etc/passwd | nawk -F: ' $4 == 70 ' { print $1 $4 $5 }
bill 70 William Philbert
paul 70 Paul Robertson
dawn 70 Dawn Stewart
$
```

In this example, the **cat** command passes the entire contents of the **/etc/passwd** file, which contains information about system users, to the **nawk** command. Because the fields in **/etc/passwd** are separated by colons, you have to change the field separator to a colon (:). Next, **nawk** searches for records in which the fourth field (working group) is 70 and prints fields 1 (login name), 4 (group identifier), and 5 (user identification). The output is three lines, representing the three users who belong to working group 70.

The default field separator is a blank space (or a tab). As the previous example illustrates, you can change it to something else (such as a colon or a slash). The default record separator is newline, meaning that a record is equivalent to s line. However, you can also change the record separator if necessary.

For example, suppose you wanted to use entire lines as fields, with five lines to a record, and a separate line that contained only the character @ as a record separator. Then you could read such a file with **nawk** in the following way:

```
$ nawk -f step FS="\n" RS="\@" lines
```

In this example, the **nawk** program is stored in a file called **step**, whereas the input file is called **lines**. The newline character is assigned to the field separator (FS) and the at sign (@) is assigned to the record separator (RS).

Assuming each record is one line, you can use the **getline** function to read the next line of input (record) and assign it to a variable. The default variable to which the record is assigned is the current record, $0. In its simplest form,

```
getline [variable]
```

the function reads the next line (record), assigns it to the variable indicated (*variable*) or implied ($0), and increments the **nawk** built-in variables NR and FNR.

The **getline** function can also read the next line (record) from another file via indirection, as shown here:

```
getline [variable] < file
```

With this format, the function reads the next line (record) of output from *command*, assigns it to the variable indicated (*variable*) or implied ($0), and increments the **nawk** built-in variables NR and FNR.

You can use a number of control statements in your **awk/nawk** programs:

break   Exit from the current **do**, **for**, or **while** loop immediately

continue   Begin the next iteration of the current **do**, **for**, or **while** loop immediately

```
do statement
   while ( condition )  Continue execution of
   statement as long as condition is true
```

exit   Leave the main section of the **awk/nawk** program and proceed immediately to the END section

exit *expr*   Exit from the **awk/nawk** program and return the value of *expr* as the exit status code (for example, **exit NR-10**)

for (*start; stop; incr*)

    statement   Begin executing *statement* with *start*, increment *incr* for the start of each new iteration, and end the loop when *stop* is no longer true. For example,

```
    { size[NR] = $3; cost[NR] = $4 }
END { for ( i=1; i<=NR; i++ )
    print size[i] "TAB" cost[i] }
```

will collect sizes and costs from the third and fourth fields in arrays size and cost; then send all elements in these arrays to the output (press the TAB key between the double quotes to insert a tab into the output)

```
for ( variable in array )
   statement
```

Execute a set of iterations of *statement*,

allowing *variable* to step through the subscripts of *array*. For example,

```
      { cost[$2] += $3; n[$2]++ }
END   { for ( variety in cost )
      print variety, "TAB",
      cost[variety]/n[variety] }
```

will collect total costs (field 3) for each variety (field 2) in an array called **cost**, along with the total number of items of each variety in another array called n; then send to the output the name of each variety, followed by its average cost (the total cost for that variety divided by the total number of items of that variety)

```
if ( expr )
   statement
```

If *expr* is true, then execute *statement*. For example,

```
if ( $6 == 0 )
   break
```

causes an exit from the current loop if the sixth field is zero.

```
if ( expr )
   statement1
else ( statement2 )
```

If *expr* is true, then execute *statement1*; if *expr* is false, then execute *statement2*. For example,

```
if ( $6 == 0 )
   break
else continue
```

causes an exit from the current loop if the sixth field is zero or the start of the next iteration if the sixth field is not zero.

next   Go on to the next input record

```
while ( expr )
   statement
```

Continue executing *statement* as long as *expr* is true. For example,

```
i = 1
```

```
while ( i <= 25 )
   print type[i+]
```

illustrates another way to construct a loop, initializing the counter at 1, then sending each element of array type up to 25 to the output

;   No statement

Now take a closer look at the **print** statement, which **awk/nawk** uses to produce output. Once again, "print" actually means "display" in the UNIX environment. At the time UNIX was originally being developed, the only output device available was a printing TeleType machine, and the only way to output information was to print it on a roll of paper. The word *print* still survives today, even though nearly all users now use video screens.

The **print** command can be used in the following constructions:

print	Output the entire record ($0)
print *expr1,expr2,...*	Output a set of expressions, by default separated by spaces and terminated with a newline
print *expr1,expr2,...* > *file*	Output a set of expressions to *file*, overwriting any existing contents
print *expr1,expr2,...* | *command*	Output a set of expressions to the standard input of *command*

The **printf** statement, borrowed from the C language, works much like **print**, except that **printf** offers more precise formatting. The **printf** statement can be used in all the constructions the **print** statement can be used in.

The **printf** statement is always followed by a pair of parentheses, which contain a set of formatting specifications, followed by the items to be printed. The formatting specifications are enclosed within a pair of double quotes and followed by a comma, which is outside the double quotes. The general format of the **printf** statement is as follows:

```
printf ("formatting", item1 item2 item3 ... )
```

The formatting section of the statement, which must be enclosed within double quotes, can contain either print specifications for items to be printed or codes for control characters. Each print specification must correspond to one item in the list that follows the comma. For example, consider the following statement:

```
printf ("%8s \t %6.2f \n ", $3 $5 )
```

In this example, \t represents a tab, \n represents a newline, %8s reserves eight columns for a string, and %6.2f reserves six columns for a floating-point number, with two of the six columns set aside for digits that follow the decimal point. Furthermore, %8s matches $3 (the first item to be printed), whereas %6.2f matches $5 (the second item). A pictorial representation of what the previous **printf** statement calls for is as follows:

_____ *tab* ___.___ *newline*
(field 3)   (field 5)

The %8s code leaves eight columns for the third field (assumed to be a string); \t provides for a tab to precede the next item; %6.2 leaves a total of six columns, including one for a decimal point and two for digits to follow, for the fifth field (assumed to be a floating-point number); finally, \n ends the line with a newline.

Each format code for an item to be printed begins with a percent sign, followed by a number to indicate the width of the field and a letter to indicate the type of information.

A numeric field code may also provide for a decimal point, along with the number of digits to follow the decimal point. For example, %8.3f provides for a total of eight columns for a floating-point number, four digits before the decimal point, the decimal point itself, and three more digits following.

Floating-point fields are justified on the decimal point; other types of numeric fields are right-justified by default. To left-justify a numeric field, insert a minus sign between the percent sign and the width of the field.

The field types supported by the **printf** statement are as follows:

c   Single character
d   Decimal integer
e   Exponential (for example, 4.123456E+10)
f   Exponential (for example, 123.123456)
g   Shorter of **e** or **f**, with leading zeroes omitted
o   Octal (base eight)
s   String
x   Hexadecimal (base sixteen)

To output a percent sign, use the notation %%.

Suppose you open a file or pipe, write information to it, and then read the new contents. Before reading the updated file, you have to close it in the **awk/nawk** program. Here is an example, using fragments from a program:

```
print >> "test"
...
close("test")
...
getline < test
```

In the first line shown, information is appended to a file called **test**. The **close** statement in the middle line is required; if it's missing, the **getline** statement in the concluding line will fail to read the appended lines.

Command Index

Index

!

for autonumbering lines in C
shell, 191
reserved Bourne shell variable, 181

!!

to reinvoke the most recent
event, 191, 219

" or '

string quoting character, 168-69,
191, 218

#

reserved Bourne shell variable,
180-81

$

reserved Bourne shell variable, 181

$HOME

home directory, 164
as environmental variable, 2
returning to, 11-12

$LOGNAME

Bourne shell variable, 148

&

at end of command line to run a
background process, 8

-

reserved Bourne shell variable, 181

.

execute command, 182, 208, 239

:

null command, 182, 239

;;

to end branch, 172, 226

>

redirection symbol, 44-45

?

reserved Bourne shell variable, 181

@

command, 197

\

character quoting symbol, 168,
190-91, 218
escape character in **awk** patterns,
244-45

^

half-space symbol, 82

^]

escape character, 113

{ and }

to enclose **awk** or **nawk** action,
246

~

with period to end a remote
session, 110

s

pace symbol, 82

A

accept command, 97, 100
Accounting information, 159,
165-66, 214
Actions in **awk** and **nawk**, 246-57
Addresses in a script, 66
alias command, 195, 209, 222-23, 239
Aliases
in the C shell, 195-96
in the Korn shell, 222-23
Arguments, command-line, 5
Arrays
awk/nawk indexed, 248
notation in Korn shell for, 234
ASCII characters, conversions to,
141-42
autoload command, 212
Autonumbering lines, 191
Autonumbering lists and footnotes,
85-86